The Flavors of bon appétit 2008

Flourless Chocolate Cake with Toasted Hazelnuts
and Brandied Cherries (page 198)

The Flavors of bon appétit 2008

from the Editors of Bon Appétit

Condé Nast Books

New York

For *Bon Appétit* Magazine

Barbara Fairchild, *Editor-in-Chief*
Tricia Callas O'Donnell, *Contributing Editor, Books*
Marcy MacDonald, *Editorial Business Director*
Carri Marks Oosterbaan, *Editorial Production Director*
Suzanne Perreault, *Editorial Production Manager*
Zoë Adnopoz, *Editorial Administrator*
Marcia Hartmann Lewis, *Editorial Support*
Susan Champlin, *Text*
Shayna Sobol, *Copy Editor*
Karen Hallal, *Research*
Elizabeth A. Matlin, *Index*

For Condé Nast Books

Lisa Faith Phillips, *Vice President and General Manager*
Deborah Williams, *Operations Director*
Helena Santini, *Editor*

Design: Monica Elias and Ph.D

Front Jacket: Herb-Rubbed Top Sirloin Steak with Peperonata (page 50)
Facing Page: Top: Crispy Eggplant Fritters with Smoked Mozzarella (page 16)
Middle: Spice-Rubbed Duck Legs Braised with Green Olives and Carrots (page 84)
Bottom: Caramel Pudding Tart with Almond Shortbread Crust (page 170)

Published by Condé Nast Books, Random House Direct, Inc., New York, New York.
A wholly owned subsidiary of Random House, Inc.

Printed in the United States of America

Library of Congress Cataloging-in-Publication Data is available upon request.

10 9 8 7 6 5 4 3 2 1

FIRST EDITION

Condé Nast Web Address: bonappetit.com
Bon Appétit Books Web Address: bonappetitbooks.com

Contents

Introduction

The exciting thing about cooking is that it's a series of surprises. It may not seem that way on a Thursday night when you're standing in the kitchen holding yet another package of skinless, boneless chicken breasts and wondering, *What on earth can I do differently with these?* Yes, even then surprise is possible if you have an open mind—and a well-stocked pantry and fridge. (You know the expression, "Luck favors the well-prepared"?) In less than half an hour and with fewer than ten ingredients, those ordinary chicken breasts can be transformed into a sensational Chicken Sauté with Wilted Endive and Brussels Sprouts (page 75) or Chicken Saltimbocca with Lemon Sauce (page 76). Surprised?

Sometimes it's the purchase of a new kitchen gadget that radically alters your thinking about food preparation: like the first time you grate Parmesan cheese or citrus rind with a razor-sharp Microplane, or use an immersion blender to whip up a creamed soup in a matter of seconds. Suddenly, cooking is *fun* again.

The first taste of a new ingredient can also open up worlds of possibility. Ever tried the peppery Japanese spice blend called *shichimi togarashi*? Once you taste it on the simple but unforgettable Salt and Pepper Oven Fries (page 141), you'll be eager to experiment with it on chicken, fish, and noodle dishes, too. Look for *shichimi* in the Asian foods section of some supermarkets, or at Japanese markets—where you're likely to come away with a basketful of other inspiring ingredients as well.

Salt and Pepper Oven Fries (page 141)

Then there's the "Aha!" moment that comes from an unexpected marriage of flavors—flavors delicious in their own right yet so extraordinary in combination that you slap your forehead and say out loud, "Why didn't I think of that?" That's what *Bon Appétit* and *The Flavors of Bon Appétit 2008* are all about.

Ginger and Pink Grapefruit Cheesecake (page 196)

The genius of *Bon Appétit* recipes (and the magazine's gifted recipe contributors) is the way in which they start with a familiar concept and subtly add new layers until the result is an astonishingly delicious surprise.

Bruschetta, for instance, is one of the most popular of contemporary appetizers. Prosciutto and Fig Bruschetta (page 18)—prepared on grilled fruit-and-nut bread that is spread with honey butter and layered with prosciutto, radicchio, and freshly grilled figs—may be one of the most exceptional versions you've ever tried.

Consider a hearty macaroni and cheese—livened up with spicy Buffalo chicken (page 122); a robust lasagna—layered with artichoke hearts and a sweet pea-ricotta cheese mixture (page 126); or Warm Doughnuts à la Mode with Bananas and Spiced Caramel Sauce (page 192). On second thought, don't consider that one—just make it.

There's a bonus to cooking with *Bon Appétit*: These recipes will inspire "Aha!" moments of your own. Once you discover that coffee, cumin, and yogurt create an amazing rub for leg of lamb (page 56), or that arugula and peaches play off each other beautifully in a salad with a creamy chive vinaigrette (page 150), or that ginger and pink grapefruit make a lively complement to rich cheesecake (page 196), all kinds of ingredient combinations begin to seem possible.

And that's when the exciting surprise of cooking begins all over again.

Watermelon-Lime Agua Fresca (page 38)

Starters

Appetizers

Soups

Beverages

Warm Asparagus Toasts with Pancetta and Vinaigrette

1 tablespoon Sherry wine vinegar
½ teaspoon Dijon mustard
3 tablespoons extra-virgin olive oil
3 tablespoons butter, melted, divided

2 ounces sliced pancetta (Italian bacon)

1 pound thick asparagus, tough ends trimmed
4 ½-inch-thick slices challah, brioche, or other egg bread, halved lengthwise

Preheat oven to 450°F. Whisk vinegar and mustard in small bowl. Gradually whisk in oil and 1 tablespoon melted butter. Season vinaigrette with salt and pepper.

Place pancetta on rimmed baking sheet. Bake until crisp, about 7 minutes.

Meanwhile, cook asparagus spears in large skillet of boiling salted water until tender, about 5 minutes. Drain asparagus; pat dry. Transfer warm asparagus to large bowl; add vinaigrette and toss to coat. Season to taste with salt and pepper. Toast bread slices and brush with remaining 2 tablespoons melted butter.

Arrange 2 toasts on each of 4 plates. Divide pancetta and asparagus among toasts. Drizzle any remaining vinaigrette over and serve.

4 SERVINGS

Golden Beet Carpaccio

- 4 medium (2½-inch diameter) golden beets, trimmed, scrubbed
- 3 tablespoons olive oil

- ½ cup very thinly sliced red onion
- ¼ cup extra-virgin olive oil
- 2 tablespoons drained capers
- 2 tablespoons minced fresh chives
- 6 cups (loosely packed) baby arugula

Here's a veggie take on classic carpaccio. Red chioggia beets would also be beautiful.

Preheat oven to 375°F. Toss beets with oil in roasting pan. Sprinkle with salt. Cover pan with foil. Roast beets until tender, about 50 minutes. Let beets stand covered at room temperature 20 minutes. Peel beets. Place in bowl; cover and chill at least 1 hour. *(Can be made 2 days ahead.)* Keep chilled.

Toss onion, oil, capers, and chives in small bowl. Season to taste with salt and pepper. Thinly slice beets. Arrange beets in concentric circles on each of 6 plates. Mound arugula atop center of beets on each. Spoon onion-caper mixture over. Sprinkle with salt and pepper.

6 SERVINGS

Caesar Salad Spring Rolls

DRESSING AND CROUTONS

- 1/4 cup mayonnaise
- 1 tablespoon finely grated Parmesan cheese
- 1 teaspoon minced anchovies
- 1/2 teaspoon fresh lemon juice

- 1 tablespoon butter
- 1/2 cup 1/4-inch cubes crustless sourdough bread

SPRING ROLLS

- 8 8 1/2-inch-diameter rice paper rounds*
- 16 paper-thin slices prosciutto (each about 8x3 inches)
- 4 large romaine lettuce leaves, cut lengthwise into 1/4-inch-wide strips
- 1 1/2 cups (packed) baby arugula leaves

FOR DRESSING AND CROUTONS: Whisk first 4 ingredients in small bowl to blend. Season dressing with salt and pepper.

Melt butter in small skillet over medium heat. Add bread cubes. Sauté until golden brown, about 4 minutes. Turn out onto paper towel. Sprinkle with salt and pepper; cool. *(Can be made 1 day ahead. Cover dressing and chill. Store croutons airtight at room temperature.)*

FOR SPRING ROLLS: Pour some warm water into large shallow dish. Submerge 1 rice paper round in water until beginning to soften, about 45 seconds. Place on sheet of parchment paper; top with 2 slices prosciutto, arranged side by side and covering most of rice paper round. Place 1/8 of lettuce and arugula down center. Tightly roll into cylinder, enclosing filling; wrap in plastic. Repeat with remaining rounds and filling. *(Can be made 4 hours ahead; chill.)*

Remove plastic from spring rolls; trim ends. Cut each into three 2-inch-long pieces; stand upright on platter. Top with dollop of dressing and croutons. Transfer to platter and serve.

A handheld hybrid of the ubiquitous salad and the popular Vietnamese appetizer.

**Thin Thai or Vietnamese wrappers, known as* banh trang, *made from rice flour; available at Asian markets.*

MAKES 24 PIECES

Zucchini Patties with Feta

- 2½ cups coarsely grated zucchini (from about 3 medium)
- 1 teaspoon salt, divided
- 1 large egg
- 1 large egg yolk
- ½ cup (or more) all purpose flour
- ½ cup crumbled feta cheese
- 1 cup chopped fresh Italian parsley
- ½ cup chopped green onions
- 1½ tablespoons chopped fresh dill

- ½ cup (about) olive oil
- ½ cup (about) corn oil

- Plain Greek yogurt

Toss zucchini and ½ teaspoon salt in large bowl. Let stand 5 minutes. Transfer to sieve. Press out excess liquid; place zucchini in dry bowl. Mix in egg, yolk, ½ cup flour, cheese, and ½ teaspoon salt. Mix in parsley, onions, and dill. If batter is very wet, add more flour by spoonfuls.

Heat 2 tablespoons olive oil and 2 tablespoons corn oil in large skillet over medium heat. Working in batches, drop batter by rounded tablespoonfuls into skillet. Fry patties until golden, 5 minutes per side, adding more olive oil and corn oil as needed. Transfer to paper towels. *(Can be made 1 day ahead. Place on baking sheet, cover, and chill. Rewarm uncovered in 350°F oven 12 minutes.)* Serve with yogurt.

MAKES ABOUT 18

Sweet-and-Sour Spareribs

2 pounds pork spareribs, well trimmed, cut into single ribs (about 8 to 9 ribs)

¾ cup water
3 tablespoons sugar
2 1-inch-diameter ½-inch-thick slices peeled fresh ginger, smashed
2 tablespoons soy sauce
2 tablespoons Shaoxing wine (Chinese rice wine)* or dry Sherry
1 tablespoon dark soy sauce*
1 tablespoon Chinkiang vinegar* or balsamic vinegar
1 tablespoon ketchup
½ teaspoon salt

Place spareribs in pot large enough to hold ribs in single layer. Add enough cold water to cover ribs. Bring to boil, spooning off any foam that rises to surface. Boil 1 minute. Transfer ribs to colander; rinse under cold water. Drain.

Wash and dry same pot. Add ¾ cup water, sugar, ginger, 2 tablespoons soy sauce, rice wine, dark soy sauce, vinegar, ketchup, and salt to pot. Stir over medium-high heat until sugar dissolves. Add spareribs to pot, turning to coat with sauce mixture (sauce will not cover ribs). Arrange spareribs in single layer in pot; bring to boil. Reduce heat to low; cover and simmer until ribs are very tender, turning ribs occasionally and adding a few tablespoons water as needed to maintain liquid level, about 2 hours. *(Can be made 1 day ahead. Chill uncovered until cold, then cover and keep chilled. Rewarm over medium heat.)*

Transfer ribs to platter. Boil sauce in pot until reduced to generous 1/2 cup, about 5 minutes. Pour sauce over spareribs and serve.

**Available at Asian markets and at specialty foods stores.*

4 SERVINGS

Ketchup might seem odd in this dish, but some say it's Asian in origin (from *ke-tsiap*, a pickled condiment sauce).

Chile-Roasted Almonds and Walnuts

- 1/4 cup extra-virgin olive oil
- 1 teaspoon dried crushed red pepper
- 1 1/2 cups whole unblanched almonds
- 1 1/2 cups walnut halves
- 1/2 cup whole blanched almonds
- 3/4 to 1 teaspoon coarse kosher salt
- Black pepper

Preheat oven to 350°F. Heat oil in large ovenproof skillet over medium heat. Add dried red pepper; cook 2 minutes. Add all nuts and stir 2 minutes. Place skillet in oven and roast nuts until fragrant and slightly darker in color, stirring occasionally, about 20 minutes. Sprinkle nuts with salt and pepper. *(Can be prepared 3 days ahead. Store airtight at room temperature.)*

MAKES 4 CUPS

Goat Cheese with Thyme, Peppercorns, and Lemon Oil

- 1 5.5-ounce log soft mild goat cheese
- 1 teaspoon pink peppercorns or peppercorn mélange, cracked
- 1 tablespoon fresh thyme leaves
- 3 tablespoons extra-virgin olive oil
- 1 teaspoon grated lemon peel
- 1/2 small garlic clove, pressed (optional)
- Sliced baguette (toasted, if desired)

Pink peppercorns and peppercorn mélange (a mixture of black, pink, green, and white peppercorns) are available at many supermarkets.

Place cheese on plate; using plastic wrap as aid, shape into 5-inch round. Sprinkle with salt, peppercorns, and thyme, and press into cheese. Mix olive oil, lemon peel, and garlic, if desired, in small bowl. Pour over cheese. Serve with baguette slices.

6 SERVINGS

Deviled Eggs with Horseradish and Black Pepper

1 dozen large eggs

6 tablespoons mayonnaise
3 tablespoons (or more) prepared horseradish
2 tablespoons sweet pickle juice from jar of sweet pickles
1 teaspoon freshly ground black pepper
1/4 teaspoon salt
24 fresh parsley leaves

Place eggs in large saucepan. Add enough cold water to cover by 1 inch. Cover pan; bring to boil. Remove pan from heat and let stand covered for 10 minutes. Drain. Let eggs stand in cold water until cold, about 30 minutes.

Peel eggs; halve lengthwise. Transfer yolks to processor. Trim small slice off bottom of egg white halves; place on tray, cavity side up. Process yolks until smooth. Add mayonnaise, 3 tablespoons horseradish, pickle juice, pepper, and salt to yolks; process until smooth. Adjust seasonings, adding more horseradish if desired. *(Can be made 1 day ahead. Cover whites and filling separately and chill.)* Transfer filling to pastry bag fitted with 1/4-inch plain tip. Pipe filling into cavities of egg whites. Garnish with parsley.

MAKES 24

Crispy Eggplant Fritters with Smoked Mozzarella

2 large eggplants (2 pounds total)
1 1/4 teaspoons salt, divided
Olive oil (for brushing and frying)

2 large eggs
3/4 cup finely grated Parmesan cheese
1 1/4 cups plain dry breadcrumbs, divided
1/4 cup finely chopped fresh Italian parsley
1 tablespoon chopped fresh thyme
1/4 teaspoon ground black pepper
1 1/2 tablespoons all purpose flour
4 ounces smoked mozzarella cheese,* cut into 1/2-inch cubes (about 20 cubes)

Preheat oven to 350°F. Cut eggplants crosswise into 1/2-inch-thick slices. Place on layers of paper towels. Sprinkle with 1 teaspoon salt; let stand 30 minutes. Brush 2 large baking sheets with oil. Pat eggplant dry; arrange in single layer on prepared sheets. Brush lightly with oil. Bake until eggplant is tender and dry, about 1 hour. Cool slightly; chop coarsely.

Whisk 1 egg, Parmesan cheese, 1/4 cup breadcrumbs, parsley, thyme, 1/4 teaspoon pepper, and 1/4 teaspoon salt in medium bowl. Stir in chopped eggplant (mixture will be soft). Spread 1 cup breadcrumbs on plate. Whisk 1 egg and flour in another bowl. Press and shape eggplant mixture into 1 1/4-inch-diameter balls. Press 1 piece smoked mozzarella into center of each ball, making sure eggplant mixture covers cheese. Dip balls, 1 at a time, into egg batter; roll in breadcrumbs to coat.

Pour enough oil into large skillet to reach depth of 1/4 inch; heat over medium-high heat. Working in batches, add balls to skillet; sauté until browned, turning often, about 4 minutes. Using slotted spoon, transfer to paper towels to drain. Sprinkle with salt and serve.

**Also called* mozzarella affumicata; *available at some specialty foods stores and at cheese shops.*

MAKES ABOUT 20

Prosciutto and Fig Bruschetta

½ cup (1 stick) butter, room temperature
½ cup plus 1 tablespoon honey

12 large fresh figs, stemmed, halved lengthwise
5 tablespoons extra-virgin olive oil, divided

2 tablespoons Sherry wine vinegar
1 shallot, minced
3 cups very thinly sliced radicchio
2 ounces thinly sliced prosciutto, cut crosswise into thin strips
¼ cup very thinly sliced fresh basil

12 ½-inch-thick slices fruit-and-nut bread (such as pecan-raisin), each cut into two 2x3-inch pieces

Using electric mixer, beat butter and 1/2 cup honey in small bowl. *(Honey-butter can be made 1 week ahead. Cover and chill. Bring to room temperature before using.)*

Prepare barbecue (medium-high heat). Place fig halves and 1 tablespoon oil in medium bowl; toss to coat. Grill figs until slightly charred, about 2 minutes per side; transfer to plate.

Whisk 1 tablespoon honey, 4 tablespoons oil, vinegar, and shallot in small bowl. Season dressing with salt and pepper. Combine radicchio, prosciutto, and basil in medium bowl. Toss with dressing. Season with salt and pepper.

Grill bread until just crisp, 1 to 2 minutes per side. Transfer to platter; brush toasts with honey-butter. Top each with radicchio mixture, then fig half and serve.

MAKES 24

A great way to show off the first-of-the-season figs. If you can't find figs, apricots would make a good substitute.

Calamari Fritti with Creamy Ponzu Dipping Sauce

- Vegetable oil (for frying)
- 6 tablespoons mayonnaise
- 2 tablespoons ponzu
- 1 1/2 tablespoons chopped fresh cilantro
- 1 1/2 teaspoons grated peeled fresh ginger
- 1 1/2 teaspoons fresh lime juice
- 3 pinches (or more) of cayenne pepper

- 1 pound cleaned calamari, thawed if frozen, bodies cut crosswise into 1/4-inch-thick rings, tentacles left whole
- 1/2 cup all purpose flour

Pour enough oil into heavy large skillet to reach depth of 2 inches. Heat oil to 375°F. Whisk mayonnaise and next 5 ingredients in small bowl for dipping sauce. Chill.

Sprinkle calamari with salt and pepper. Place flour in medium bowl. Working in batches, toss calamari rings and tentacles in flour to coat, then fry in oil until golden and crisp, turning occasionally, about 1 minute. Using slotted spoon, transfer calamari to paper towels to drain. Sprinkle with salt; serve immediately with dipping sauce.

4 TO 6 SERVINGS

Asian ingredients update this Italian appetizer. Specialty foods stores and Asian markets carry *ponzu*, a Japanese sauce made with lemon juice, rice vinegar, soy sauce, *mirin*, and seaweed.

Steamed Artichokes with Salsa Verde

- ½ teaspoon fennel seeds
- ½ cup fresh Italian parsley leaves
- 2 tablespoons drained capers, rinsed
- 3 tablespoons chopped shallot
- 2 garlic cloves, coarsely chopped
- 1½ tablespoons fresh tarragon leaves
- 1 anchovy fillet
- Pinch of dried crushed red pepper
- ½ cup extra-virgin olive oil
- 2 tablespoons whipping cream
- 2 teaspoons Sherry wine vinegar

- 4 medium globe artichokes
- ½ lemon

Heat small skillet over medium heat. Add fennel seeds and toast until aromatic and beginning to darken, about 2 minutes. Transfer seeds to processor. Add parsley, capers, shallot, garlic, tarragon, anchovy, and crushed red pepper to processor. Puree until coarse paste forms, scraping down sides occasionally. Transfer to medium bowl. Whisk in oil, cream, and vinegar. Season with salt and pepper. *(Salsa verde can be made 2 hours ahead. Let stand at room temperature.)*

Lay 1 artichoke on its side and cut off top third; cut off stem at base of artichoke. Using scissors, cut top ½ inch off each remaining leaf. Rub all cut surfaces with lemon, squeezing slightly to release juice. Repeat with remaining artichokes.

Place rack on bottom of large pot. Add enough water just to touch rack. Bring to boil. Place artichokes on rack in pot. Reduce heat to medium, cover, and steam artichokes until tender, adding more water if necessary, about 30 minutes.

Transfer 1 artichoke to each of 4 plates. Cool 10 minutes. Divide salsa verde among 4 small bowls and serve alongside artichokes.

4 SERVINGS

Bresaola with Shaved Brussels Sprouts and Horseradish

In Italy, thin slices of *bresaola* are typically served as an antipasto. In this recipe, the thinly sliced meat is topped with a crunchy brussels sprout salad.

- 3 tablespoons olive oil
- 3 tablespoons Sherry wine vinegar
- 3 tablespoons minced shallot
- 12 large brussels sprouts, trimmed
- 12 thin slices bresaola* (about ¼ pound)
- Grated fresh horseradish

Whisk oil, vinegar, and shallot in small bowl. Season dressing with salt and pepper. Using mandoline or V-slicer, thinly slice brussels sprouts. Place 4 cups shaved brussels sprouts in large bowl. Add dressing; toss to coat. Season with salt and pepper.

Arrange 3 bresaola slices over each of 4 plates. Divide brussels sprout salad among plates, mounding in center so bresaola is visible. Sprinkle horseradish over brussels sprout salad and serve.

**Air-cured beef; available in the deli section of some supermarkets and at specialty foods stores.*

4 SERVINGS

Crostini with Feta-Chile Spread

- 3 large fresh poblano chiles*
- 1 jalapeño chile
- 4 ounces feta cheese (about ½ cup)
- ¼ cup low-fat sour cream
- 1 tablespoon finely chopped fresh dill
- 2 teaspoons fresh lemon juice

- 18 ½-inch-thick baguette slices
- Extra-virgin olive oil

Prepare barbecue (medium heat). Char poblano and jalapeño chiles until blackened all over. Wrap chiles in paper bag and let stand 15 minutes. Peel, seed, and coarsely chop 2 poblano chiles and jalapeño chile; transfer to processor. Add feta cheese, sour cream, chopped fresh dill, and lemon juice to processor; puree until smooth. Season with salt and pepper. Cover and chill until firm enough to spread, about 2 hours. Peel, seed, and thinly slice remaining poblano chile. *(Can be made 1 day ahead. Keep spread chilled. Cover and chill sliced chile.)*

Prepare barbecue (medium-high heat). Brush 1 side of baguette slices with extra-virgin olive oil. Grill oiled side of bread until toasted, about 2 minutes. Transfer toasts to platter. Spoon about 2 teaspoons chile spread over each toast, top with thinly sliced poblano chile, and serve.

**Poblano chiles are often called pasillas. They're available at some supermarkets and at specialty foods stores and Latin markets.*

6 SERVINGS

Melted Rosemary Brie on Apple Wedges

- 2 large Granny Smith or Fuji apples, cored, cut into ½-inch-thick slices
- 1 10-ounce piece Brie, rind trimmed, cheese cut into thin slices
- Chopped fresh rosemary

Arrange apples on baking sheet. Top each with slice of Brie. Sprinkle with rosemary and freshly ground black pepper. *(Can be made 1 hour ahead. Cover; let stand at room temperature.)*

Preheat broiler. Broil apples uncovered until cheese melts, moving sheet for even cooking, about 1 minute. Transfer to platter; serve hot.

8 SERVINGS

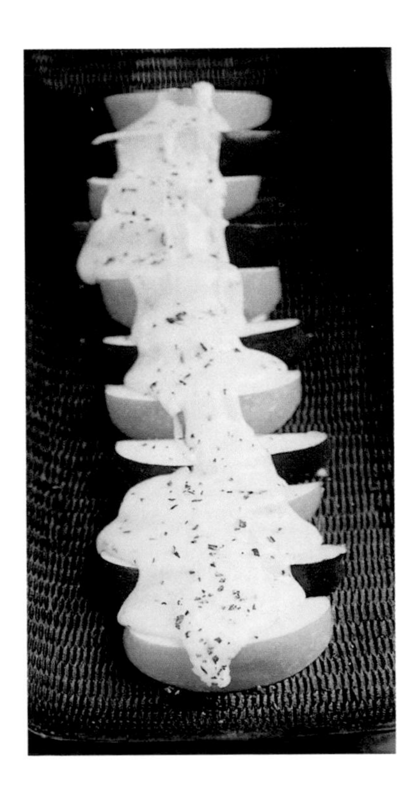

Parsnip Soup with Corned Beef and Cabbage

- 3 ⅛-inch-thick slices cooked corned beef (4 ounces), fat trimmed, chopped (3 tablespoons reserved, divided)
- 2 Turkish bay leaves
- 2 large parsnips (about 13 ounces), peeled, coarsely chopped
- 2 cups chopped onions
- 3 cups (or more) low-salt chicken broth
- 3 large savoy cabbage leaves, center ribs removed
- ¼ cup heavy whipping cream

Sauté 2 tablespoons corned beef fat and bay leaves in large saucepan over medium-high heat until fat renders, about 2 minutes. Stir in parsnips and onions. Add 3 cups broth. Cover; simmer until parsnips are tender, about 10 minutes.

Meanwhile, cut cabbage and corned beef slices crosswise into very thin strips. Melt 1 tablespoon fat in medium skillet over medium-high heat. Add cabbage and corned beef. Sprinkle with salt and pepper. Toss until cabbage wilts, about 3 minutes.

Working in batches, puree soup with bay leaves and cream in blender until smooth. Return to same pan. Rewarm soup, thinning with more broth if too thick. Season with salt and pepper. Ladle into bowls. Mound corned beef and cabbage in center.

4 SERVINGS

Zucchini, Potato, and Cilantro Soup

- 3 tablespoons butter
- 1 tablespoon (or more) chopped jalapeño chile with seeds
- ¼ teaspoon (generous) fennel seeds
- 1 7- to 8-ounce Yukon Gold potato, peeled, cut into ½-inch cubes
- 16 to 18 ounces zucchini (about 4 medium), trimmed, cut into ½-inch rounds
- 1 cup chopped green onions
- 2½ cups low-salt chicken broth
- ½ cup (packed) fresh cilantro
- 1 teaspoon (or more) fresh lime juice

Melt butter in heavy large saucepan over medium-high heat. Add chile and fennel seeds; stir 30 seconds. Add next 3 ingredients; sauté 2 minutes. Add broth and bring to boil. Reduce heat to medium-low, cover, and simmer until vegetables are tender, about 15 minutes.

Puree soup in batches in blender, adding cilantro and 1 teaspoon lime juice to first batch. Return puree to same pan. Season to taste with salt, pepper, and more lime juice, if desired. Rewarm, if necessary, and serve.

4 SERVINGS

White Bean Soup with Chile Paste

CHILE PASTE

2 dried ancho chiles,* stemmed, seeded
1 dried chile de árbol,* stemmed, seeded

1½ cups water
1 tablespoon dark brown sugar
3 tablespoons vegetable oil

SOUP

2 cups dried Great Northern beans

2 tablespoons (¼ stick) butter
2 celery stalks, finely chopped
1 large carrot, finely chopped
1 large white onion, finely chopped
1 large garlic clove, minced
8 cups (or more) water
2½ teaspoons ground cumin
2 teaspoons ground coriander
½ cup whipping cream

FOR CHILE PASTE: Place chiles in bowl; add enough water to cover. Let stand at room temperature overnight. Drain.

Boil 1½ cups water, sugar, and chiles in small saucepan until 2 tablespoons liquid remain, about 15 minutes. Transfer to processor; puree until smooth. With machine running, gradually add oil. Season with salt and pepper. *(Can be made 3 days ahead.)* Cover; chill.

FOR SOUP: Place beans in large pot. Add enough water to cover by 4 inches. Let soak overnight.

Drain beans. Melt butter in same pot over medium-high heat. Add celery, carrot, onion, and garlic; cook until soft, stirring often, about 15 minutes. Add beans and 8 cups water. Bring to boil, reduce heat to low, and cook until beans are soft, stirring occasionally, about 1½ hours. Stir in cumin and coriander; cool. Working in batches, puree soup in blender, adding water by

¼ cupfuls if too thick. Return to same pot. Stir in cream. Season with salt and pepper. *(Can be made 1 day ahead. Cover; chill.)*

Rewarm soup. Divide among bowls. Drizzle with chile paste. Swirl paste into soup; serve.

**Sold at many supermarkets and at specialty foods stores and Latin markets.*

8 SERVINGS

The beans and the chiles need to soak overnight, so start this the day before.

Spinach and Mint Soup

Paprika oil adds a hit of color—and flavor.

- ½ cup extra-virgin olive oil, divided
- 1½ cups chopped onion
- 1 9- to 10-ounce russet potato, peeled, thinly sliced
- 2 large garlic cloves, peeled
- 4½ cups (or more) low-salt chicken broth
- 3 green onions, chopped
- 2 10-ounce packages frozen chopped spinach, thawed, drained very well
- 1 cup chopped fresh mint, divided
- ⅓ cup chopped fresh cilantro

- 2 teaspoons Hungarian sweet paprika

Heat ¼ cup oil in large saucepan over medium heat. Add onion; sauté until tender, about 8 minutes. Add potato and garlic; sauté 5 minutes. Add 4½ cups broth and green onions; bring to boil. Cover and simmer until potato is tender, about 15 minutes. Add spinach, ¾ cup mint, and cilantro. Simmer soup 1 minute.

Puree soup in blender in batches; return to same pot. Thin with more broth by ¼ cupfuls, if desired. Season soup with salt and pepper. *(Can be made 1 day ahead. Chill until cold, then cover and keep chilled. Rewarm before serving.)*

Heat remaining ¼ cup oil in small skillet over low heat. Mix in paprika; cook 1 minute. Ladle soup into bowls. Drizzle with paprika oil; garnish with remaining ¼ cup mint.

8 SERVINGS

Vanilla-Date Breakfast Smoothie

1 cup nonfat yogurt
1 cup nonfat milk
1 cup (packed) pitted Medjool dates (about 9 ounces)
½ teaspoon vanilla extract
2 cups ice cubes

Puree yogurt, milk, dates, and vanilla in blender until smooth. Add ice cubes; puree until mixture is thick and smooth. Divide between 2 glasses and serve.

MAKES 2

Zinfandel Sangria with Brandy and Orange

- 2¼ cups water
- 2¼ cups sugar
- 6 750-ml bottles Zinfandel
- 2¼ cups brandy
- 1½ cups triple sec or other orange liqueur
- 1½ cups orange juice
- 6 apples, cored, thinly sliced
- 4 nectarines or peaches, pitted, thinly sliced
- 4 lemons, cut into thin rounds

Stir 2¼ cups water and 2¼ cups sugar in medium saucepan over medium-high heat until sugar dissolves. Cool simple syrup. Combine Zinfandel, brandy, triple sec, orange juice, and 3 cups simple syrup in very large container. Add apples, nectarines, and lemons. Refrigerate sangria until cold, at least 3 hours and up to 1 day. Ladle sangria and fruit into pitchers. Serve over ice.

20 TO 24 SERVINGS

Ginger Lime Cosmopolitan

The tart citrus vodka and lime juice are balanced by the spice of the fresh ginger.

- 1 lime, quartered
- 4 tablespoons sugar, divided
- ½ cup citrus-flavored vodka
- 2 tablespoons fresh lime juice
- 2 teaspoons freshly grated peeled ginger
- 1 cup ice
- 2 lime slices

Run 1 lime quarter around rims of 2 Martini glasses. Place 3 tablespoons sugar on small plate. Dip rims into sugar. Place all lime quarters, 1 tablespoon sugar, vodka, lime juice, and ginger in cocktail shaker. Mash with muddler or end of wooden spoon until lime wedges are crushed. Add ice; shake well. Strain mixture between prepared glasses, garnish with lime slices, and serve.

2 SERVINGS

Watermelon-Cucumber Margarita

- 1½ cups 1-inch chunks rindless watermelon
- 6 ⅛-inch-thick slices English hothouse cucumber
- 15 large fresh mint leaves
- ½ cup 100% blue agave silver tequila
- ¼ cup fresh lime juice
- 3 tablespoons Simple Syrup (see recipe)
- 1 tablespoon Cointreau or other orange liqueur
- 2 cups ice cubes, divided
- 2 small watermelon triangles, each skewered with 1 cucumber round (for garnish)
- 2 fresh mint sprigs (for garnish)

Place first 3 ingredients in medium bowl. Press firmly on solids with muddler or back of wooden spoon until mashed. Mix in tequila, lime juice, Simple Syrup, and Cointreau, then 1 cup ice. Stir to blend well. Strain into large glass measuring cup. Divide remaining ice between 2 tall glasses. Pour mixture over. Garnish with watermelon skewers and mint sprigs.

MAKES 2

Simple Syrup

- 2 cups sugar
- 2 cups water

Stir sugar and water in medium saucepan over medium heat until sugar disolves. Increase heat and bring to boil. Reduce heat and simmer 3 minutes. Cool. *(Can be made 2 weeks ahead. Refrigerate in airtight containers.)*

Grapefruit-Pomegranate Cocktail

- 7 tablespoons water
- 5 tablespoons pomegranate juice
- ¼ cup sugar
- 4 teaspoons honey

- 1½ cups vodka
- ¾ cup fresh grapefruit juice
- ¼ cup fresh lime juice
- 18 fresh mint leaves plus 6 sprigs for garnish
- Ice cubes

Bring first 4 ingredients to boil in small saucepan, stirring to dissolve sugar. Cool. *(Can be made 1 day ahead. Cover and refrigerate.)*

Combine pomegranate mixture, vodka, grapefruit juice, lime juice, and mint leaves in large pitcher. Fill pitcher with ice. Stir vigorously. Strain drink into Martini glasses. Garnish each glass with mint sprig and serve.

MAKES 6

Drunken Pear

Ice cubes
½ cup bourbon
6 tablespoons pear liqueur
2 tablespoons peach liqueur
2 tablespoons fresh lime juice
4 dashes angostura bitters
2 ¼-inch-thick slices fresh pear (for garnish)

Fill cocktail shaker with ice. Add next 5 ingredients. Shake 15 seconds. Strain into Martini glasses. Garnish with pear slices.

MAKES 2

This recipe calls for bitters, a bittersweet liquid made from a spirit (usually rum) infused with bark, roots, plants, and aromatic herbs.

Milkie Way Malt

2½ cups vanilla bean ice cream
⅓ cup whole milk
1 tablespoon malted milk powder
1 tablespoon milk chocolate chips
1 tablespoon caramel sauce plus additional for drizzling

Chocolate syrup
Malted milk balls, coarsely crushed

Place two 8-ounce glasses in freezer to chill. Combine first 4 ingredients and 1 tablespoon caramel sauce in blender; process on high speed until thick and smooth, about 30 seconds.

Squirt chocolate syrup and caramel sauce into both glasses; split malt mixture between glasses. Top with malted milk balls.

2 SERVINGS

Strawberry Milk Shakes

1 cup Strawberry Syrup (see recipe) plus additional for drizzling
1 cup whole milk
2 pints strawberry ice cream, slightly softened
4 strawberries with stems (optional; for garnish)

Place four 12-ounce glasses in freezer for 1 hour.

Place 1 cup Strawberry Syrup, 1 cup milk, and 1 pint ice cream in blender; puree until smooth. Add second pint of ice cream and puree until almost smooth. Divide mixture among frozen glasses. Drizzle each with some Strawberry Syrup, garnish with strawberry, if desired, and serve with spoon and straw.

4 SERVINGS

Strawberry Syrup

1 pound sliced hulled strawberries
½ cup water
½ cup sugar
⅓ cup corn syrup
Pinch of salt
2 tablespoons lemon juice

Bring first 5 ingredients to boil in large saucepan over medium-high heat, stirring until sugar dissolves. Boil uncovered 10 minutes, stirring occasionally and adjusting heat to prevent mixture from boiling over. Add 2 tablespoons lemon juice. Strain, pressing on solids. Cover and chill syrup. *(Can be made 1 week ahead. Keep chilled.)*

MAKES 2½ CUPS

White Peach Summer Bellini

2 medium-size very ripe unpeeled white peaches, halved, pitted
2 tablespoons (or more) lemon juice
2 tablespoons (or more) Simple Syrup (see recipe on page 34)
1 750-ml bottle chilled Prosecco

Puree peaches, lemon juice, and syrup in blender. Taste; add more syrup or lemon juice, if desired. Pour 2 tablespoons puree into each of 6 Champagne flutes. Fill with Prosecco.

MAKES 6

Bridal Shower Lunch for 12

Caesar Salad Spring Rolls
(page 12)

Phyllo-Cheese Triangles

White Peach Summer Bellini
(double recipe; at left)

Cauliflower and Caramelized Onion Tart
(double recipe; page 106)

Bibb Lettuce and Fresh Herb Salad with Roquefort
(page 159)

Sourdough Rolls

Sauvignon Blanc, Iced Tea, and *Sparkling Water*

Chocolate Strawberry Shortcakes
(double recipe; page 194)

Coffee

Napa Valley Winter Punch

- 1½ 3- to 4-inch-long cinnamon sticks
- 2 whole nutmegs
- 1½ tablespoons whole allspice berries
- ⅓ cup sugar

- 2 cups Simple Syrup (see recipe on page 34)

- 2¼ cups Charbay Rum or 10 Cane Rum
- 1¼ cups fresh lemon juice
- 1¼ cups fresh orange juice
- 1 teaspoon bitters
- 1 block of ice
- Lemon and orange slices

Place cinnamon and nutmeg in resealable plastic bag; crack into pieces using mallet or rolling pin. Transfer to spice grinder. Add allspice; blend to coarse powder. Transfer 1 tablespoon to shallow dish; mix in ⅓ cup sugar. Set spiced sugar aside.

Stir remaining spice powder in medium saucepan over medium-high heat until just beginning to smoke, about 2 minutes. Remove from heat; cool 5 minutes. Repeat heating and cooling process 3 more times until spices are fragrant but not burned. Add Simple Syrup; bring to boil. Reduce heat; simmer 5 minutes. Strain through sieve into bowl. Cool.

Mix ¾ cup spice syrup, rum, lemon juice, orange juice, and bitters in punch bowl. Add ice and citrus slices. Rub 1 orange slice around rim of 8 glasses to moisten; dip glasses into spiced sugar. Place glasses around punch bowl.

8 SERVINGS

Watermelon-Lime Agua Fresca

- 1 3-ounce piece of ginger, peeled, grated

- 10 cups 1-inch pieces peeled watermelon (from about 8-pound watermelon), seeded, divided
- 3 cups cold water, divided
- ⅓ cup fresh lime juice
- ¼ cup (or more) sugar

- Ice cubes
- Lime wedges

Wrap grated ginger in cheesecloth; twist at both ends to squeeze out juice. Or put grated ginger in fine-mesh sieve and press to release juices. Set aside.

Place 2½ cups watermelon and ¾ cup cold water in blender. Puree until smooth. Pour agua fresca into large pitcher. Repeat 3 more times with remaining watermelon and cold water. Add lime juice, 1/4 cup sugar, and ginger juice to pitcher and stir to blend. Add more sugar by tablespoonfuls, if desired. Refrigerate until well chilled, at least 3 hours. *(Can be made 8 hours ahead. Keep chilled.)* Stir before serving.

Fill glasses with ice cubes; pour agua fresca over. Garnish each glass with lime wedge and serve.

MAKES ABOUT 8 CUPS

It's an all-purpose refresher—drink it straight, top with sparkling water, or spike with vodka, gin, or tequila. If you don't want to make your own fresh ginger juice, look for it in natural foods stores.

Tangerine-Ginger Caipirinhas

- 3 small unpeeled tangerines, chopped, seeded
- 12 teaspoons sugar
- 3 teaspoons grated peeled ginger
- 12 tablespoons tangerine juice
- 1½ cups cachaça (Brazilian sugarcane liquor) or vodka

Divide tangerines among 6 tumblers. Add 2 teaspoons sugar and 1/2 teaspoon grated peeled ginger to each glass. Crush ingredients in bottom of glass with muddler or handle of wooden spoon. Top each drink with 2 tablespoons tangerine juice and 1/4 cup cachaça or vodka. Fill glasses with ice cubes, stir, and serve.

6 SERVINGS

The Caipirinha is Brazil's most popular cocktail. The drink is traditionally made with limes, but tangerines provide a nice change of pace.

Grill-Roasted Clam Linguine (page 125)

Main Courses

Meats

Poultry

Seafood

Meatless

Pasta & Pizza

Pan-Grilled Beer-Marinated Hanger Steak

- 1/4 cup soy sauce
- 2 tablespoons olive oil
- 3 large garlic cloves, minced
- 2 teaspoons Dijon mustard
- 2 teaspoons chopped fresh rosemary
- 2 teaspoons Worcestershire sauce
- 2 teaspoons coarsely ground black pepper
- 1/2 cup dark lager beer (such as bock, märzen, or Samuel Adams Black Lager)
- 2 1/2 pounds trimmed hanger steaks (about 3 pieces)

Nonstick vegetable oil spray

Whisk first 7 ingredients in medium bowl, then whisk in beer. Pour marinade into large resealable plastic bag. Add steaks, seal bag, and chill 1 day, turning bag occasionally.

Spray large ridged skillet or grill pan with nonstick spray and heat over medium-high heat. Remove steaks from marinade and pat dry; discard marinade. Place steaks in hot skillet and cook until well browned and thermometer inserted into center registers 125°F to 130°F for medium-rare, about 5 minutes per side. Transfer steaks to carving board and let rest 5 minutes.

Slice steaks thinly across grain. Arrange on platter; spoon any accumulated juices over and serve.

6 SERVINGS

Named because it hangs between the rib and the loin, hanger steak delivers an intense hit of beefy flavor. Marinating and pan-searing are the best ways to prepare it. Hanger steak absorbs marinade well and is tender enough for quick, high-heat cooking.

Spiced Beef Stew with Carrots and Mint

- 2 tablespoons olive oil, divided
- 12 ounces beef tenderloin, cut into 1-inch cubes
- 1 cup sliced shallots (about 3 large)
- 8 ounces peeled baby carrots
- 2 teaspoons ground cumin
- 1½ teaspoons pumpkin pie spice
- ⅛ teaspoon cayenne pepper
- 1 tablespoon all purpose flour
- 2½ cups beef broth
- ⅓ cup chopped fresh mint, divided
- Prepared couscous

Heat 1 tablespoon oil in large nonstick skillet over high heat. Sprinkle beef with salt and pepper. Add beef to skillet and sauté until cooked to desired doneness, about 2 minutes for medium-rare. Using slotted spoon, transfer beef to bowl. Add remaining 1 tablespoon oil to skillet. Add shallots and carrots and sauté until golden, about 3 minutes. Add all spices; stir 30 seconds. Sprinkle flour over; stir 30 seconds. Stir in broth and bring to boil. Reduce heat to medium; simmer until carrots are just tender, about 8 minutes. Return beef to skillet; cook until sauce thickens slightly, about 1 minute. Season stew to taste with salt and pepper. Stir in ¼ cup chopped mint. Spoon couscous into bowls. Spoon stew over couscous. Sprinkle with remaining chopped fresh mint and serve.

2 SERVINGS

Grilled Steak Kebabs with Orange and Hoisin Glaze

Nonstick vegetable oil spray
½ cup frozen orange juice concentrate, thawed
½ cup hoisin sauce*
2 tablespoons chili powder
1½ tablespoons olive oil
2 teaspoons (packed) finely grated orange peel

1½ pounds beef tenderloin steaks (about 1¼ inches thick), cut into 20 cubes
3 ⅓-inch-thick orange slices

Chopped green onions

Spray grill rack with nonstick spray and prepare barbecue (medium-high heat). Whisk juice concentrate, hoisin, chili powder, oil, and orange peel in medium bowl; season sauce with salt and pepper.

Place beef in large bowl. Sprinkle with salt and pepper; toss to coat. Add ¼ cup sauce; toss well. Let stand 5 minutes. Cut each orange slice into 6 wedges. Alternate 5 beef cubes and 4 orange wedges on each of 4 metal skewers.

Grill kebabs to desired doneness, brushing with more sauce and turning occasionally, about 10 minutes for medium-rare.

Place 1 skewer on each of 4 plates; sprinkle with onions. Serve with remaining sauce.

**Available in the Asian foods section of many supermarkets and at Asian markets.*

4 SERVINGS

Grilled Flank Steak with Sautéed Beet Greens and Creamy Horseradish Beets

BEETS

8 medium beets with green tops
2 tablespoons olive oil

⅓ cup crème fraîche or sour cream
3 tablespoons prepared white horseradish
2 tablespoons fresh lemon juice
1 tablespoon minced shallot

FLANK STEAK

4 tablespoons olive oil, divided
2 tablespoons Dijon mustard

1 tablespoon Worcestershire sauce
1 tablespoon chopped fresh rosemary
1 garlic clove, minced
½ teaspoon ground black pepper
1 1½-pound flank steak

Nonstick vegetable oil spray

You will need to buy eight beets for their greens, but you'll use only four of the roots. If the beet juice turns your hands red, rub them with salt or lemon juice to remove the stain.

FOR BEETS: Preheat oven to 375°F. Trim green tops from beets; cut off stems and discard, reserving greens. Gently scrub 4 beets and set aside (reserve remaining beets for another use). Toss beets with 2 tablespoons oil in roasting pan. Sprinkle with salt. Cover pan with foil. Bake until beets are tender, about 50 minutes. Let beets stand covered at room temperature 20 minutes. Peel beets; cut into ½-inch cubes.

Whisk crème fraîche, horseradish, lemon juice, and minced shallot in medium bowl. Add beets and toss to coat. Season to taste with salt and pepper. Let stand at room temperature at least 20 minutes. *(Can be made 2 hours ahead. Let stand at room temperature.)*

FOR FLANK STEAK: Whisk 2 tablespoons olive oil, Dijon mustard, Worcestershire sauce, chopped rosemary, minced garlic, and ground black pepper in 13x9x2-inch glass baking dish. Add steak; turn to coat. Cover and chill at least 1 hour and up to 2 hours. Spray grill rack with nonstick spray. Prepare barbecue (medium-high heat). Remove steak from marinade; sprinkle with salt and pepper. Grill steak to desired doneness, about 5 minutes per side for medium-rare. Remove from grill; let stand 5 minutes.

Meanwhile, heat remaining 2 tablespoons oil in heavy large skillet over medium-high heat. Add reserved beet greens; sauté until wilted, about 3 minutes. Remove from heat, cover, and let stand 3 minutes. Thinly slice steak crosswise. Divide steak among 6 plates; surround with sautéed beet greens. Mound horseradish beets alongside.

6 SERVINGS

Wood-Smoked Tri-Tip with Sicilian Herb Sauce

- 3 tablespoons fresh thyme leaves
- 2 garlic cloves, peeled
- 1½ teaspoons dried oregano
- 1 teaspoon coarse kosher salt or coarse sea salt
- 2 tablespoons fresh lemon juice
- ½ cup extra-virgin olive oil

- 1 well-trimmed 2½- to 2¾-pound tri-tip beef roast

- 3 cups oak, mesquite, or hickory wood chips, soaked in water 1 hour and drained

Blend thyme leaves, garlic cloves, dried oregano, and coarse salt in mini processor until garlic is finely chopped. With processor running, gradually add lemon juice, then olive oil. Season herb sauce to taste with pepper and transfer to bowl. *(Can be made 1 day ahead. Cover and chill. Bring to room temperature before using.)*

Sprinkle roast generously on both sides with salt and freshly ground black pepper. Let stand at least 30 minutes and up to 2 hours.

Prepare barbecue (medium-high heat). IF USING GAS GRILL: Wrap wood chips in foil; pierce foil all over with fork. Remove top grill rack, place foil packet directly on burner, and replace grill rack. Place roast over packet and grill uncovered 6 minutes (wood in foil will begin to smoke). Turn roast over. Move to spot on grill where heat is indirect and medium-hot. Cover grill and cook until thermometer inserted into thickest part of roast registers 128°F to 135°F for medium-rare, turning roast occasionally, about 13 minutes. IF USING

CHARCOAL GRILL: Sprinkle wood chips over coals and place roast on rack. Cook roast uncovered 7 minutes. Turn roast over. Move roast to spot on grill where heat is indirect and medium-hot. Cover grill and cook until thermometer inserted into thickest part of roast registers 128°F to 135°F for medium-rare, turning roast occasionally, about 13 minutes.

Transfer roast to platter. Let stand 10 minutes. Thinly slice roast across grain. Serve, passing sauce separately.

6 SERVINGS

The simple herb, lemon, and garlic sauce is called *salmoriglio* in Sicily.

Feta Burgers with Grilled Red Onions

These newfangled burgers are stuffed with feta cheese. Pressing the center of the raw hamburger to form a slight indentation prevents the burger from puffing up in the center when cooking.

- 3 pounds lean ground beef
- 1 cup (packed) crumbled feta cheese
- 2 teaspoons dried oregano
- 1½ teaspoons salt
- 1½ teaspoons ground black pepper

- 8 large garlic cloves, peeled
- ½ cup plus 1 tablespoon extra-virgin olive oil

- Nonstick vegetable oil spray
- 2 medium red onions, peeled, each cut crosswise into 4 slices
- 8 hamburger buns

- 2 large tomatoes, each cut crosswise into 4 slices

Break up beef in large bowl. Sprinkle feta, oregano, salt, and pepper over; toss. Divide into 8 portions; form each into 4½-inch patty, pressing in center to form slight indentation. *(Can be made 1 day ahead.)* Cover; chill.

Puree garlic in processor. With machine running, gradually add ½ cup oil; process 30 seconds. *(Can be made 1 day ahead)*. Cover; chill.

Spray grill rack with nonstick spray. Prepare barbecue (medium-high heat). Brush onion with 1 tablespoon oil; sprinkle with salt and pepper. Place burgers and onions on grill. Cover; cook 5 minutes. Turn; cook until onions are charred in spots and burgers are medium-well, about 4 minutes longer. Transfer to plate. Brush cut sides of buns with garlic oil. Place buns, cut side down, on grill; toast about 1 minute. Turn; cook until heated, about 1 minute.

Place burgers on bun bottoms. Top each with onion, tomato, and bun top and serve.

8 SERVINGS

Herb-Rubbed Top Sirloin Steak with Peperonata

PEPERONATA

- 3 tablespoons extra-virgin olive oil
- 2 small red onions (about 12 ounces total), halved, sliced crosswise
- 2 pounds mixed red and yellow bell peppers (about 4 large), cut lengthwise into ½-inch-wide strips
- ¼ teaspoon dried crushed red pepper
- Coarse kosher salt
- 3 tablespoons red wine vinegar
- 2 tablespoons salt-packed capers, rinsed, drained, or 2 tablespoons capers in brine, drained
- 1 tablespoon chopped fresh oregano
- 1 tablespoon chopped fresh thyme

STEAK

- 1 tablespoon chopped fresh oregano
- 1 tablespoon chopped fresh thyme
- 1 tablespoon freshly cracked black pepper
- 1½ teaspoons coarse kosher salt
- 1 3- to 3¼-pound top sirloin steak, 2 to 2½ inches thick

Extra-virgin olive oil (for drizzling)

FOR PEPERONATA: Heat olive oil in heavy large pot over medium heat. Add onions; sauté until almost tender, about 6 minutes. Mix in bell peppers and crushed red pepper; sprinkle lightly with coarse kosher salt. Reduce heat to low, cover, and cook until peppers are tender and silky, stirring occasionally, about 35 minutes. Stir in red wine vinegar, capers, oregano, and thyme. Increase heat to medium; stir uncovered 3 minutes. Season peperonata to taste with coarse salt and pepper. Transfer to bowl and cool to room temperature. *(Can be made 3 days ahead. Cover and refrigerate. Bring to room temperature before serving.)*

FOR STEAK: Mix oregano, thyme, pepper, and salt in small bowl. Sprinkle evenly over both sides of steak. Place on large plate; cover and refrigerate at least 4 hours and up to 6 hours. Let stand at room temperature 1 hour before grilling.

Prepare barbecue (medium-high heat). Drizzle both sides of steak lightly with olive oil. Grill steak to desired doneness, about 15 minutes per side for medium-rare, or 17 minutes per side for medium. Transfer steak to cutting board; let rest 5 minutes. Cut steak crosswise into ¼- to ⅓-inch-thick slices.

Arrange steak slices on platter; surround with peperonata and serve.

6 TO 8 SERVINGS

Porcini-Crusted Filet Mignon with Tarragon-Chive Butter

- ¾ cup (1½ sticks) butter, room temperature
- 3 tablespoons chopped fresh chives
- 1½ tablespoons chopped fresh tarragon
- 1 small garlic clove, pressed
- 1 ½-ounce package dried porcini mushrooms*

- 6 1-inch-thick filet mignon steaks

Mix first 4 ingredients in small bowl for herb butter. Season to taste with salt and pepper. Process dried mushrooms in spice grinder to fine powder. Transfer powder to plate. Sprinkle steaks with salt and pepper. Press steaks into porcini powder to coat both sides well.

Melt 2 tablespoons herb butter in heavy large nonstick skillet over medium heat. Add steaks to skillet and cook to desired doneness, about 6 minutes per side for medium-rare. Transfer to plates. Spoon rounded tablespoon herb butter atop each steak and serve.

**Available in the produce section of many supermarkets and at specialty foods stores and Italian markets.*

6 SERVINGS

Buffalo Meatloaf with Spinach and Roasted Baby Potatoes

- 1 pound baby Yukon Gold or Dutch yellow potatoes
- 5 tablespoons olive oil, divided

- 1½ cups chopped crimini (baby bella) mushrooms
- 1 cup chopped red onion
- 1 tablespoon chopped fresh sage
- 1 tablespoon chopped fresh thyme

- 1 pound ground buffalo meat*
- 1 large egg
- ¾ cup tomato sauce, divided
- ½ cup panko (Japanese breadcrumbs)**
- ½ teaspoon salt
- ½ teaspoon cracked black pepper
- ¼ teaspoon dried crushed red pepper

- 1 garlic clove, pressed
- 2 5-ounce bags fresh spinach

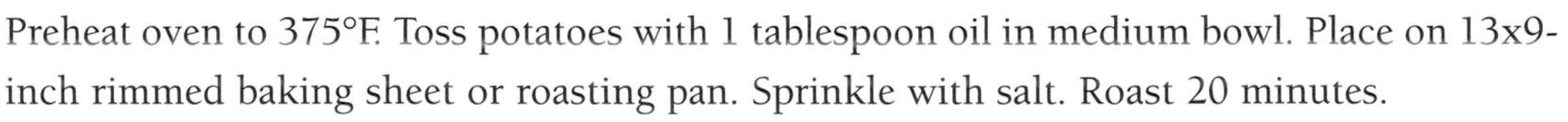

Preheat oven to 375°F. Toss potatoes with 1 tablespoon oil in medium bowl. Place on 13x9-inch rimmed baking sheet or roasting pan. Sprinkle with salt. Roast 20 minutes.

Meanwhile, heat 2 tablespoons oil in medium skillet over medium heat. Add mushrooms and onion; sauté until mushrooms are beginning to brown and onion is translucent, about 4 minutes. Remove from heat; mix in sage and thyme. Cool slightly.

Mix buffalo, mushroom mixture, egg, ½ cup tomato sauce, panko, salt, and black pepper in large bowl. Push potatoes to sides of baking sheet; shape buffalo mixture into 6x3-inch loaf in center of sheet. Roast 30 minutes. Combine ¼ cup tomato sauce and red pepper in small bowl. Pour over top of meatloaf. Roast 20 minutes longer. Remove from oven; let rest while preparing spinach.

Heat remaining 2 tablespoons oil and garlic in large pot over medium-high heat. Add spinach and toss until wilted, about 3 minutes. Season to taste with salt. Slice meatloaf; serve potatoes and spinach alongside.

**Available at specialty foods stores and some farmers' markets.*

***Available in the Asian foods section of some supermarkets and at Asian markets.*

4 TO 6 SERVINGS

Grilled Veal Chops and Radicchio with Lemon-Caper Sauce

- 4 tablespoons extra-virgin olive oil, divided
- 1½ tablespoons white balsamic vinegar
- 1½ tablespoons drained capers
- 1½ tablespoons chopped fresh Italian parsley
- 1¼ teaspoons finely grated lemon peel
- 1 small garlic clove, minced

- 2 8- to 9-ounce veal rib chops (each about ¾ inch thick)
- 6 radicchio leaves

Perfect with roasted potatoes, a simple green salad, and a bottle of Chardonnay.

Whisk 3 tablespoons olive oil and next 5 ingredients in small bowl to blend. Season sauce to taste with salt and pepper. (*Can be made 2 hours ahead. Let stand at room temperature.*)

Prepare barbecue (medium-high heat) or heat heavy large skillet over medium-high heat. Brush veal chops with remaining 1 tablespoon olive oil; sprinkle with salt and pepper. Place veal chops on grill or in skillet and cook to desired doneness, about 6 minutes per side for medium. Transfer to platter. Brush radicchio lightly with some of sauce. Place leaves on grill or in batches in skillet and cook just until slightly wilted but not brown, pressing lightly to flatten, about 45 seconds to 1 minute per side.

Divide radicchio and veal chops between plates. Spoon sauce over and serve.

2 SERVINGS

Braised Veal Breast with Herbs, Pernod, and Tomatoes

- 1 4¾- to 5-pound large end of veal breast (about 8 bones), cut between bones into individual ribs
- 1 tablespoon chopped fresh thyme
- 1 tablespoon chopped fresh sage
- 2 tablespoons olive oil

- 1 large onion, halved, thinly sliced
- 8 large garlic cloves, chopped
- 2 large shallots, sliced
- 3 anchovy fillets, chopped
- 1 cup dry white wine
- ¼ cup Pernod or other anise-flavored liqueur
- 1 14½-ounce can diced tomatoes in juice
- 1 cup low-salt chicken broth
- 1 tablespoon chopped fresh tarragon
- 1 10-ounce bag pearl onions, peeled
- 1 cup brine-cured green olives (such as picholine; about 6 ounces)

- 2 tablespoons grated lemon peel

Sprinkle veal ribs on all sides with salt, pepper, thyme, and sage. Heat oil in heavy large wide pot over medium-high heat. Add half of ribs and sauté until brown, turning occasionally, about 10 minutes. Transfer ribs to bowl. Repeat with remaining ribs. Reduce heat to medium-low.

Add onion, garlic, and shallots to pot. Cover and cook until soft, occasionally scraping up any browned bits, about 8 minutes. Mix in anchovy fillets; cook 1 minute. Add white wine and Pernod. Increase heat and boil mixture 3 minutes. Add diced tomatoes with juice, chicken broth, and chopped fresh tarragon; stir to blend. Add veal and any accumulated juices from bowl, arranging veal in single layer in pot. Bring to simmer. Reduce heat to medium-low, cover, and simmer until veal is tender, turning veal occasionally, about 1¾ hours. Add peeled pearl onions and green olives to pot. Cover and simmer until pearl onions are tender, about 25 minutes longer. *(Braised veal can be made 2 days ahead. Cool slightly. Chill uncovered until cold, then cover and keep refrigerated. Rewarm before continuing.)*

Using tongs, transfer veal to plate. Tilt pot and spoon off fat from top of sauce; discard fat. Boil sauce until thick enough to coat spoon, about 5 minutes. Mix in grated lemon peel. Return veal to sauce and simmer until heated through and flavors blend, about 5 minutes. Season to taste with salt and pepper. Transfer veal to large shallow bowl and serve.

4 SERVINGS

Chinese Char Siu Grilled Lamb Chops

3 tablespoons hoisin sauce*
3 tablespoons soy sauce
2 tablespoons Shaoxing wine (Chinese rice wine) or dry Sherry
1 tablespoon sugar
1 teaspoon Chinese five-spice powder**
½ teaspoon salt
18 rib lamb chops (about 3 pounds), well trimmed

2 tablespoons honey
1 tablespoon water

Whisk first 6 ingredients in small bowl. Transfer to large resealable plastic bag. Add lamb; seal bag and turn to coat. Marinate in refrigerator at least 4 hours or overnight.

Prepare barbecue (medium-high heat). Drain lamb, leaving some marinade clinging. Grill lamb until slightly charred and cooked to desired doneness, about 2½ minutes per side for medium-rare. Transfer to platter.

Stir honey and 1 tablespoon water in small skillet over medium heat until warm. Brush over lamb chops.

**Available in the Asian foods section of many supermarkets and at Asian markets.*
***A spice blend that usually contains ground fennel seeds, Szechuan peppercorns, cinnamon, star anise, and cloves; available in the spice section of most supermarkets.*

6 SERVINGS

Cumin-and-Coffee Roasted Leg of Lamb

¾ cup plain whole-milk yogurt
1 tablespoon ground cumin
1 tablespoon (packed) dark brown sugar
1 teaspoon instant espresso powder
⅛ teaspoon ground cloves
1 3¾-pound boneless leg of lamb, well-trimmed, butterflied

Position rack in top third of oven and preheat to 475°F. Stir yogurt, cumin, brown sugar, espresso powder, and cloves in small bowl until sugar dissolves. Place lamb, fat side up, on rimmed baking sheet. Sprinkle generously with salt and pepper. Spread 1/3 of yogurt mixture evenly over. Turn lamb over. Sprinkle generously with salt and pepper. Spread evenly with remaining yogurt mixture.

Roast lamb until thermometer inserted into thickest part registers 130°F for medium-rare, about 25 minutes. Transfer to platter. Let rest 10 minutes. Slice thinly and serve.

6 TO 8 SERVINGS

Spicy Lamb with Charred Eggplant Puree and Pita

- 6 12- to 14-ounce eggplants
- 2 large garlic cloves, peeled
- 3/4 teaspoon salt
- 1 1/2 cups plain Greek yogurt or drained plain whole-milk yogurt
- 7 8-ounce lamb shoulder blade chops (about 3/4 inch thick), trimmed and boned, meat cut into 3/4-inch cubes
- 1/2 teaspoon dried crushed red pepper

Chopped fresh mint or Italian parsley
Warm pita bread wedges

Char eggplants directly over gas flame or in broiler until blackened on all sides and very tender in center, about 20 minutes. Cool; cut open. Spoon flesh into sieve set over bowl; discard skins. Drain at least 1 hour and up to 3 hours.

Transfer eggplant to bowl and mash. Chop garlic with salt and mash to paste; mix into eggplant. Mix in yogurt. Season with salt and pepper. *(Can be made 1 day ahead. Cover; chill.)*

Heat large nonstick skillet over high heat. Sprinkle lamb with salt and pepper; add to skillet in single layer. Sprinkle with dried crushed pepper. Cover, reduce heat to medium-low, and cook lamb until tender and brown, turning occasionally and adding water by tablespoonfuls if very dry, about 45 minutes. *(Can be made 1 day ahead. Cover lamb in skillet and chill. Rewarm over low heat.)*

Warm eggplant over low heat; spoon into dish. Spoon lamb and any juices over. Sprinkle with parsley. Serve with pita.

6 SERVINGS

Pan-Grilled Lamb with Walnut-Mint Pesto

LAMB

4 9- to 10-ounce (round-bone) lamb shoulder chops
2 tablespoons olive oil
4 large fresh rosemary sprigs
4 garlic cloves, peeled, crushed

PESTO

1 cup fresh Italian parsley
1 cup fresh mint leaves
½ cup walnuts, lightly toasted
⅓ cup olive oil
½ small garlic clove, peeled
2¼ teaspoons fresh lemon juice

FOR LAMB: Combine all ingredients in large bowl; turn lamb to coat with oil. Let stand at room temperature 1 hour. *(Can be made 1 day ahead. Cover; chill. Let stand at room temperature 1 hour before cooking.)*

FOR PESTO: Blend first 5 ingredients in processor to coarse puree, occasionally scraping down sides of processor. Mix in lemon juice. Season with salt and pepper. Transfer to bowl. *(Can be made 1 day ahead. Cover; chill.)*

Heat large griddle or large skillet over high heat. Add lamb chops with rosemary-garlic mixture. Cook to desired doneness, about 4 minutes per side for medium-rare. Transfer to plates; top with pesto.

4 SERVINGS

Lamb shoulder chops are widely available and are less expensive than lamb rib chops. These are terrific with roasted potatoes and sautéed spinach.

Slow-Roasted Lamb Shoulder with Pancetta

- 8 garlic cloves, peeled
- 4 ounces pancetta (Italian bacon), diced
- 3 tablespoons chopped fresh rosemary
- 2 teaspoons cracked black pepper
- 1 4-pound rolled boned lamb shoulder (about 7 pounds before boning), excess fat trimmed

Because of its ample fat, lamb shoulder can be open-roasted rather than braised and still remain moist—as long as it's roasted at a low temperature.

Drop garlic down feed tube of mini processor; chop finely. Scrape down bowl sides. Add pancetta, rosemary, and pepper; blend to coarse paste. Using small sharp knife, make 1/2-inch-deep slits all over lamb and fill each with pancetta paste. Spread any remaining paste over outside of lamb. Place lamb, seam side down, in roasting pan. *(Can be prepared 1 day ahead. Cover with plastic wrap and chill.)*

Preheat oven to 300°F. Roast lamb uncovered until very tender and thermometer inserted into center registers 170°F, about 5 hours. Transfer to platter; let rest 15 minutes.

Cut lamb crosswise into 1/2-inch-thick slices. Transfer to platter. Pour pan juices into bowl. Remove and discard fat from surface. Spoon pan juices over lamb.

8 SERVINGS

Rosemary-Roasted Rack of Lamb and Cherry Tomatoes

- 1 2-pound rack of lamb (about 8 ribs)
- 3 tablespoons olive oil, divided
- 3 teaspoons chopped fresh rosemary, divided
- 2 12-ounce containers cherry tomatoes

Preheat oven to 425°F. Rub lamb with 1 tablespoon oil; sprinkle with 1½ teaspoons rosemary, then salt and pepper. Place on large rimmed baking sheet. Place 2 tablespoons oil, 1½ teaspoons rosemary, and tomatoes in large bowl. Sprinkle with salt and pepper and toss to coat; scatter around lamb.

Roast lamb and tomatoes until thermometer inserted into thickest part of lamb registers 135°F for medium-rare, about 30 minutes. Let rest 10 minutes. Cut lamb between bones into individual chops. Arrange on platter with tomatoes.

4 SERVINGS

Roasted Herb-Stuffed Leg of Lamb

- ½ cup finely chopped fresh mint plus whole sprigs for garnish
- ½ cup chopped fresh Italian parsley
- ⅓ cup olive oil
- 6 garlic cloves, minced
- 1 tablespoon minced fresh rosemary
- 1 6-pound boned and butterflied leg of lamb (about 7 pounds before boning)
- Coarse kosher salt
- ½ cup dry white wine
- ½ cup beef broth or water

Stir chopped mint and next 4 ingredients in small bowl. Place lamb, boned side up, on work surface. Sprinkle with salt and pepper. Spread with herb mixture. Roll up from long side; tie at 2-inch intervals. Rub lamb with salt and pepper. *(Can be made 1 day ahead. Cover; chill.)*

Preheat oven to 450°F. Place lamb in roasting pan. Roast uncovered until thermometer inserted into thickest part registers 130°F to 135°F for medium-rare, about 50 minutes. Transfer to platter; let rest 15 minutes. Add wine and broth to pan. Stir up browned bits over high heat. Pour pan juices into small bowl.

Remove strings from lamb; cut crosswise into ½-inch-thick slices. Place lamb on platter; garnish with mint sprigs. Serve lamb with pan juices.

8 SERVINGS

Saturday Night Dinner for 8

Warm Asparagus Toasts with Pancetta and Vinaigrette
(double recipe; page 10)

Assorted Cheeses and Olives

Sauvignon Blanc

Roasted Herb-Stuffed Leg of Lamb
(at left; pictured at left)

Warm New Potatoes, Cherry Tomatoes, and Green Beans with Fresh Basil
(page 136)

Grilled Eggplant Sprinkled with Feta Cheese

Pinot Noir

Mascarpone Tart with Honey, Oranges, and Pistachios
(page 184)

Roasted Lamb Chops with Charmoula and Skillet Asparagus

CHARMOULA

1 tablespoon cumin seeds
1½ cups (lightly packed) fresh Italian parsley leaves
½ cup (lightly packed) fresh mint leaves
½ cup (lightly packed) fresh cilantro leaves
2 large garlic cloves
1 tablespoon smoked paprika* or Hungarian sweet paprika
1 teaspoon coarse kosher salt
¼ teaspoon cayenne pepper
6 tablespoons extra-virgin olive oil, divided
1 tablespoon fresh lemon juice

LAMB

8 1¼- to 1½-inch-thick lamb loin chops (about 2⅔ pounds)

1 tablespoon butter
1 tablespoon extra-virgin olive oil
1½ pounds thin asparagus, trimmed, peeled, tops cut into 3-inch-long pieces, stalks cut into ½-inch pieces
3 tablespoons chopped shallot
1 teaspoon finely grated lemon peel

FOR CHARMOULA: Heat small skillet over medium heat. Add cumin seeds and toast until aromatic and slightly darker, stirring occasionally, about 2 minutes. Transfer to processor. Add parsley leaves and next 6 ingredients to processor. Using on/off turns, process until coarse paste forms. With machine running, gradually add 4 tablespoons oil. Transfer 2 tablespoons charmoula to small bowl; whisk in lemon juice and remaining 2 tablespoons oil. Cover and chill to serve with lamb.

FOR LAMB: Transfer remaining charmoula to large resealable plastic bag. Add lamb chops; seal bag and turn to coat well. Chill at least 4 hours and up to 24 hours. Let lamb and charmoula sauce in bowl stand at room temperature 1 hour.

Preheat oven to 500°F. Line rimmed baking sheet with foil. Place rack on prepared baking sheet. Place lamb on rack and sprinkle with salt and pepper. Roast until thermometer inserted into center registers 130°F for medium-rare, about 13 minutes. Transfer lamb to platter. Tent with foil and let rest 5 minutes.

Meanwhile, melt butter with 1 tablespoon oil in heavy large skillet over high heat. Add asparagus and sauté until tender, stirring often, about 3 minutes. Add shallot and lemon peel. Sauté 1 minute. Season to taste with salt and pepper.

Place 2 lamb chops on each of 4 plates. Divide asparagus among plates. Drizzle lamb and asparagus with charmoula sauce, passing remaining sauce alongside.

**Sometimes labeled Pimentón Duke or Pimentón de La Vera Duke; available at some supermarkets and at specialty foods stores.* Δ

4 SERVINGS

Charmoula **is a zesty herb and lemon sauce from North Africa.**

Barbecued Pork Sandwiches with Pickled Red Onion

ONION

1 red onion, halved, thinly sliced
1½ cups boiling water
1 cup plus 2 tablespoons orange juice
6 tablespoons distilled white vinegar
½ teaspoon (scant) salt

VINAIGRETTE

1 garlic clove, peeled
½ teaspoon smoked salt or coarse kosher salt
3 tablespoons purchased tomato-based barbecue sauce
2 tablespoons orange juice
2 tablespoons fresh lime juice
½ cup olive oil

PORK

1 tablespoon coarsely ground black pepper
1 tablespoon smoked paprika*
1 teaspoon smoked salt or coarse kosher salt
2 1-pound pork tenderloins

Nonstick vegetable oil spray

6 large onion rolls, split, toasted

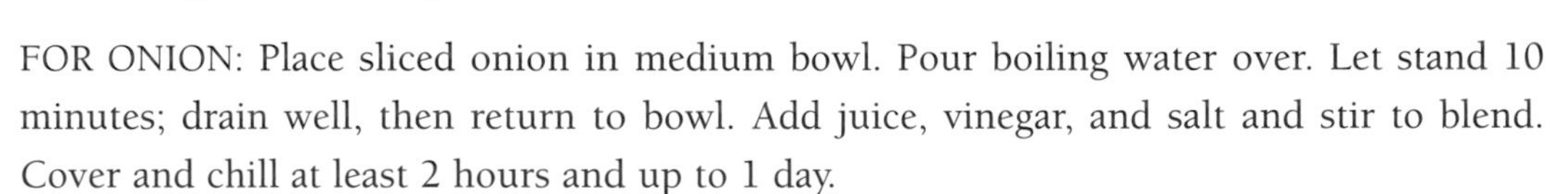

FOR ONION: Place sliced onion in medium bowl. Pour boiling water over. Let stand 10 minutes; drain well, then return to bowl. Add juice, vinegar, and salt and stir to blend. Cover and chill at least 2 hours and up to 1 day.

FOR VINAIGRETTE: Chop garlic with salt to paste; scrape into small bowl. Add barbecue sauce, orange juice, and lime juice to bowl. Gradually whisk in oil. Season with pepper.

FOR PORK: Blend pepper, smoked paprika, and salt in small bowl. Sprinkle seasoning mix evenly over both tenderloins. Let stand at least 30 minutes and up to 2 hours. Spray grill rack with nonstick spray. Prepare barbecue (high heat). Grill tenderloins uncovered 5 minutes, rolling over to sear all sides. Cover grill and continue to cook until thermometer inserted into thickest part of pork registers 145°F, turning often and moving to cooler part of grill as needed, about 15 minutes longer. Transfer to cutting board; let rest 10 minutes.

Thinly slice pork. Mound on roll bottoms. Top with well-drained onions, then drizzle with vinaigrette. Cover with roll tops and serve, passing extra onions and vinaigrette .

**Sometimes labeled Pimentón Duke or Pimentón de La Vera Duke; available at some supermarkets and at specialty foods stores.*

6 SERVINGS

Grilled Pork Chops with Tomatillo Salsa

12 tomatillos* (about 1 pound), husked, rinsed
4 garlic cloves, peeled
2 jalapeño chiles
2/3 cup finely chopped white onion
2/3 cup (lightly packed) chopped fresh cilantro

6 1¼-inch-thick pork rib chops (14 ounces each with bone)
1 garlic clove, peeled, halved
Coarse kosher salt
Extra-virgin olive oil (for brushing)
12 corn or flour tortillas

Preheat broiler. Place tomatillos, garlic, and jalapeños on rimmed baking sheet. Broil until tender and slightly charred, turning occasionally, about 7 minutes for garlic and 8 minutes for tomatillos and jalapeños. Transfer to plate and let stand until cool enough to handle. Stem and seed jalapeños. Place tomatillos, garlic, jalapeños, onion, and cilantro in processor. Puree until almost smooth. Season with salt and pepper. *(Can be made 1 day ahead. Cover and chill. Return salsa to room temperature before serving.)*

Prepare barbecue (medium-high heat). Rub both sides of pork chops with halved garlic clove. Sprinkle with kosher salt and pepper; brush with oil. Grill until just cooked through, about 8 minutes per side. Transfer to plate; let rest 10 minutes. Grill tortillas 1 minute per side. Serve chops with tortillas and salsa.

**Tomatillos are available at some supermarkets and at Latin markets.*

6 SERVINGS

Southwestern Dinner for 6

Crostini with Feta-Chile Spread
(page 23)

Grilled Pork Chops with Tomatillo Salsa
(at left; pictured at left)

Grilled Garlic-Marinated Baby Zucchini
(page 142)

Mâche and Avocado Salad with Tortilla Strips
(page 151)

Tempranillo

Lime Granita
(page 225)

Pine Nut Cookies

Tequila

Pork Shanks with Prosciutto and Porcini Mushrooms

1 ounce dried porcini mushrooms*
1 cup boiling water

4 whole fresh pork shanks with rind (each 1¼ to 1½ pounds)
4 tablespoons olive oil, divided

1 large onion, chopped
1 cup chopped carrots
1 cup chopped leek (white and pale green parts only)
½ cup chopped celery
2 ounces prosciutto, chopped
6 garlic cloves, chopped
1 cup dry white wine
1 cup low-salt chicken broth
3 teaspoons chopped fresh sage, divided
2 teaspoons chopped fresh rosemary, divided

Chopped fresh Italian parsley

Place porcini mushrooms in small bowl. Pour 1 cup boiling water over and let stand until mushrooms soften, at least 30 minutes. Drain and chop mushrooms; reserve soaking liquid.

Preheat oven to 325°F. Sprinkle pork with salt and pepper. Heat 3 tablespoons oil in heavy large wide pot over medium-high heat. Add pork, in batches if necessary, and sauté until brown on all sides, about 15 minutes. Transfer pork to rimmed baking sheet.

Spoon off and discard all but 2 tablespoons fat from pot. Reduce heat to medium. Add onion, carrots, leek, celery, and prosciutto. Cover and cook until vegetables are soft and beginning to color, stirring occasionally, about 10 minutes. Mix in garlic and chopped porcini. Add wine and bring to boil, scraping up any browned bits. Add broth and reserved mushroom soaking liquid, leaving any sediment in bowl. Mix in 1 teaspoon sage and 1 teaspoon rosemary. Return pork and any accumulated juices to pot, arranging in single layer.

Bring pork mixture to boil, cover pot, and place in oven. Braise pork until very tender, turning over every 30 minutes, about 1 hour 30 minutes. *(Can be made 2 days ahead. Cool slightly. Refrigerate uncovered until cold, then cover and keep refrigerated. Simmer until just warm before continuing.)*

Preheat oven to 425°F. Transfer pork to rimmed baking sheet. Brush with 1 tablespoon oil; sprinkle with 2 teaspoons sage, 1 teaspoon rosemary, and pepper. Roast pork until browned, about 20 minutes. Meanwhile, tilt pot and spoon any fat from surface of sauce. Boil until sauce coats spoon lightly, about 7 minutes. Season with salt and pepper. Spoon sauce onto large shallow platter. Top sauce with pork, sprinkle with parsley, and serve.

**Sold in the produce section of many supermarkets and at specialty foods stores and Italian markets.*

4 SERVINGS

Pork Rib Roast with Fig and Pistachio Stuffing

⅓ cup coarse kosher salt
¼ cup (packed) golden brown sugar
¼ cup honey
6 5-inch-long fresh rosemary sprigs
4 garlic cloves, peeled, smashed
½ teaspoon dried crushed red pepper
6 cups cold water, divided

2 3-pound center-cut bone-in pork rib roasts (about 5 bones each)

Fig and Pistachio Stuffing (see recipe)

Stir first 6 ingredients and 4 cups water in large saucepan over medium heat until salt and sugar dissolve. Remove from heat and add remaining 2 cups cold water. Cool brine to room temperature.

Place 1 pork rib roast in each of 2 large resealable plastic bags. Divide brine and seasoning equally between bags. Chill 12 to 16 hours. Remove pork from brine. Rinse; pat dry with paper towels. Let stand at room temperature 1 hour.

Preheat oven to 325°F. Heat heavy large skillet over medium-high heat. Place 1 pork roast, fat side down, in skillet and cook until brown, about 5 minutes. Transfer roast to rimmed baking sheet, fat side up. Repeat with second pork roast. Arrange roasts with ribs meeting in center of sheet. Roast until thermometer inserted into center of pork registers 145°F, about 1½ hours. Let rest 15 minutes.

Carve 6 chops from roast. Serve with Fig and Pistachio Stuffing.

The pork and figs need to marinate overnight, so be sure to begin one day ahead.

Fig and Pistachio Stuffing

5 ounces dried figs, trimmed, quartered (about 1 cup)
½ cup sweet white wine (such as Muscat or Essensia)

8 cups 1-inch cubes country-style white bread (about 12 ounces)

4 tablespoons (½ stick) butter
1 large onion, chopped (about 2 cups)
3 celery stalks, chopped
2 garlic cloves, minced
2 teaspoons chopped fresh rosemary
1 cup lightly toasted unsalted pistachios, chopped
¾ cup low-salt chicken broth

Place figs and wine in small bowl. Cover and let soak overnight.

Preheat oven to 350°F. Arrange bread cubes in single layer on rimmed baking sheet and place in oven until dry, about 15 minutes. Cool.

Reduce oven temperature to 325°F. Butter 11x7x2-inch baking dish. Melt butter in heavy large skillet over medium heat. Add onion, celery, garlic, and rosemary. Sprinkle with salt and pepper. Cover skillet and cook vegetables until soft, stirring occasionally, about 15 minutes. Transfer to large bowl. Add figs with soaking liquid, bread cubes, nuts, and broth to vegetables; toss stuffing. Transfer to prepared baking dish. *(Can be made 2 hours ahead. Let stand at room temperature.)*

Cover dish tightly with foil. Bake stuffing, covered, 45 minutes. Uncover and bake stuffing until beginning to brown, about 20 minutes.

6 SERVINGS

Roasted Pork Loin with Poached Plums

PLUMS

- 6 sweet firm red or black plums (such as Burgundies, Satsumas, or El Dorados; about 2 pounds), quartered, pitted
- 2 cups Pinot Gris or Viognier
- 1 cup dry red wine
- 2 whole star anise*
- ½ cinnamon stick
- ¼ cup plus 1¼ teaspoons sugar, divided
- 2 cups low-salt chicken broth
- 5 fresh thyme sprigs plus 1 teaspoon finely chopped thyme, divided
- 2 tablespoons chopped shallot

PORK

- 2 1¼-pound pork tenderloins
- 3 tablespoons olive oil, divided
- 2 teaspoons chopped fresh thyme
- 2 garlic cloves, minced

Chopped fresh chives

FOR PLUMS: Combine first 5 ingredients and 1/4 cup sugar in heavy large saucepan; bring to boil, stirring until sugar dissolves. Reduce heat; simmer until plums are tender, about 20 minutes. Transfer plums to platter. Strain wine mixture. Return strained liquid to same saucepan. Add broth, thyme sprigs, and shallot.

Boil until sauce is reduced to 1 cup, about 25 minutes. Strain; stir in 1 1/4 teaspoons sugar and chopped thyme. Season with salt and pepper. *(Can be made 1 day ahead. Cover plums and sauce separately; chill. Bring plums to room temperature; rewarm sauce over medium heat.)*

FOR PORK: Preheat oven to 400°F. Brush pork with 1 tablespoon oil; sprinkle with thyme, garlic, salt, and pepper. Heat remaining 2 tablespoons oil in large ovenproof skillet over medium-high heat. Add pork and cook until brown on all sides, turning often, about 5 minutes. Transfer skillet to oven: roast pork until thermometer inserted into center registers 140°F, about 20 minutes. Remove skillet from oven and let pork stand 10 minutes. Cut pork crosswise into 1/2-inch-thick slices. Serve with poached plums and sauce. Sprinkle with chopped chives.

**Brown, star-shaped seedpods; available in the spice section of some supermarkets and at specialty foods stores and Asian markets.*

6 SERVINGS

Pork Medallions with Chili-Maple Sauce

- 1 12-ounce pork tenderloin
- 1/2 teaspoon Chinese five-spice powder*
- 1 tablespoon vegetable oil
- 3/4 cup low-salt chicken broth
- 1 1/2 tablespoons pure maple syrup
- 1 tablespoon chili-garlic sauce
- 1 green onion, chopped

Cut tenderloin crosswise into 6 slices. Using meat mallet, pound medallions between 2 sheets of plastic wrap to 1/2-inch thickness. Sprinkle with salt, pepper, and five-spice powder.

Heat oil in large skillet over high heat. Add pork; cook until brown and cooked through, about 3 minutes per side. Transfer to platter. Add next 3 ingredients to skillet. Boil until reduced to scant 1/4 cup, about 2 minutes. Pour sauce over pork; sprinkle with green onion.

**Available in the spice section of most supermarkets.*

2 SERVINGS

Farmers' Market Dinner for 6

Golden Beet Carpaccio
(page 11)

Chardonnay

Roasted Pork Loin with Poached Plums
(opposite; pictured opposite)

Frisée and Fresh Herb Salad with Kumquats and Shiitake Mushrooms
(page 161)

Rice Pilaf

Pinot Noir

Panna Cotta Parfaits with Raspberry Compote
(page 210)

Cuban-Spiced Chicken Thighs with Chorizo and Rice

1/4 cup fresh lime juice
1/4 cup chopped fresh cilantro stems
2 tablespoons olive oil
1 tablespoon finely grated lime peel
1 tablespoon chopped fresh thyme
2 teaspoons chopped seeded jalapeño chile
2 teaspoons Hungarian sweet paprika
2 teaspoons ground black pepper
1 teaspoon ground cumin
1/2 teaspoon salt
1/4 teaspoon ground allspice
10 chicken thighs with skin and bone (about 4 1/2 pounds)

1 tablespoon olive oil
1/2 pound fully cooked Spanish chorizo or Portuguese linguiça sausage links, cut into 1/4-inch-thick rounds
2 cups finely chopped onions
1/2 cup chopped red bell pepper
3 garlic cloves, chopped
2 cups arborio rice or short-grain white rice
2 1/2 cups (or more) low-salt chicken broth
2 medium tomatoes, diced
2 teaspoons Hungarian sweet paprika
1/4 teaspoon saffron threads

1 canned piquillo pepper or 1 whole canned pimiento, cut into thin strips

1/2 cup coarsely chopped fresh cilantro
Lime wedges

Whisk first 11 ingredients in medium bowl for marinade. Place chicken in large resealable plastic bag; add marinade. Seal bag; turn several times to coat chicken. Refrigerate chicken at least 4 hours and up to 1 day, turning bag occasionally. Using tongs, transfer chicken from bag to plate, allowing excess marinade to drip back into bag. Reserve marinade.

Heat 1 tablespoon oil in heavy large wide pot over medium heat. Add chorizo and sauté until beginning to brown and fat begins to render, about 3 minutes. Using slotted spoon, transfer chorizo to medium bowl. Increase heat to medium-high. Add half of chicken, skin side down, to pot. Sauté until brown, about 5 minutes per side. Transfer to plate. Repeat with remaining chicken. Pour off all but 3 tablespoons fat from pot; discard excess fat. Add chopped onions; sauté 4 minutes, scraping up any browned bits. Add chopped bell pepper and chopped garlic. Sauté until onions are translucent, about 2 minutes. Mix in rice, stirring to blend with vegetables. Add 2 1/2 cups broth, tomatoes with any juice, paprika, saffron, and reserved marinade. Bring to boil, stirring to blend. Return chicken, chorizo,

and any accumulated juices to pot, pressing chicken partially into rice.

Reduce heat to low, cover, and simmer 15 minutes. Arrange piquillo pepper strips over chicken pieces. Cover and continue to simmer until rice is tender and chicken is cooked through, adding more broth by 1/4 cupfuls if rice is dry, about 10 minutes longer. Season to taste with salt and pepper.

Transfer rice and chicken to large shallow bowl. Garnish with cilantro and lime wedges and serve.

6 SERVINGS

Chicken thighs have dark meat that's moist, flavorful, and almost impossible to overcook. Here, stewing gives the meat big flavor and helps balance the dish. Uncork a Merlot to go with it.

Grilled Tandoori-Style Chicken and Mangoes with Mango Jasmine Rice

- ½ cup chopped fresh cilantro
- ½ cup chopped fresh parsley
- 4 garlic cloves
- 1 tablespoon ground cumin
- 1 tablespoon sweet paprika
- 1 tablespoon coarse kosher salt
- ½ teaspoon cayenne pepper
- ½ cup olive oil
- 1 cup plain whole-milk yogurt
- ¼ cup fresh lemon juice

- 2 2½-pound chickens, quartered

- 2 large ripe mangoes, peeled; 1 cut into ½-inch-thick slices, 1 cut into ½-inch cubes

- 2 cups jasmine rice
- 3 cups water
- ½ cup pine nuts, toasted

- 6 fresh cilantro sprigs

Puree first 7 ingredients in processor. With machine running, gradually add oil through feed tube and process until blended. Transfer 1/4 cup herb mixture to small bowl; reserve. Add yogurt and lemon juice to remaining mixture in processor and blend.

Place chicken in 13x9x2-inch glass baking dish. Pour yogurt mixture over chicken; turn to coat. Cover and refrigerate 1 hour.

Prepare barbecue (medium heat). Place chicken, skin side down, on grill. Cover; grill until chicken is cooked through, turning every 5 minutes, about 30 minutes total. Grill mango slices 2 minutes per side.

Meanwhile, combine rice, 3 cups water, and reserved 1/4 cup herb mixture. Bring to boil. Reduce heat to low; cover and simmer until tender, about 15 minutes. Remove from heat; let stand, covered, 5 minutes. Fold in mango cubes and pine nuts.

Arrange chicken on large platter; garnish with grilled mango slices and cilantro sprigs. Serve mango jasmine rice alongside.

8 SERVINGS

Mangoes are used two ways in this Indian dish—grilled with the chicken and tossed into rice. To dice a mango, slice off sides of fruit (start each cut about a half-inch to the side of the stem to avoid the pit). Cut a grid through the flesh of each half down to the peel. Push up on peel side so that the cubes stick out. Slice off the cubes at their base.

Chicken Sauté with Wilted Endive and Brussels Sprouts

- 2 skinless boneless chicken breast halves
- 2 teaspoons chopped fresh herbs (such as tarragon and chives)
- 4 tablespoons (1/2 stick) butter, divided
- 5 large brussels sprouts, quartered
- 2 large heads of Belgian endive, quartered lengthwise
- 1/4 cup low-salt chicken broth
- 2 teaspoons white balsamic vinegar

Using meat mallet, pound chicken breast halves between sheets of plastic wrap to 1/2-inch thickness. Sprinkle chicken with 1 teaspoon chopped fresh herbs, salt, and pepper.

Melt 2 tablespoons butter in large nonstick skillet over medium-high heat. Add chicken and sauté until cooked through, about 3 minutes per side. Transfer chicken to plate and tent with foil. Add remaining 2 tablespoons butter to same skillet and cook until brown, about 1 minute. Add brussels sprouts and endive and sauté until golden, adding broth to moisten, about 3 minutes. Add vinegar; toss to coat. Season with salt and pepper. Mix in remaining 1 teaspoon herbs. Divide vegetables between plates. Top with chicken and serve.

2 SERVINGS

Chicken Saltimbocca with Lemon Sauce

4 skinless boneless chicken breast halves
8 large fresh sage leaves
8 thin prosciutto slices (about 3 ounces)
½ cup plus 2 teaspoons all purpose flour

1 tablespoon butter
1½ tablespoons olive oil

2 tablespoons dry white wine
½ cup low-salt chicken broth
2 tablespoons fresh lemon juice

Place chicken between 2 sheets of plastic wrap on work surface. Using mallet, pound chicken to 1/3-inch thickness. Sprinkle chicken with salt and pepper. Place 2 sage leaves atop each chicken breast half. Top each chicken breast with 2 prosciutto slices, pressing to adhere. Spread 1/2 cup flour on plate. Turn chicken in flour to lightly coat both sides.

Melt butter with oil in large nonstick skillet over medium-high heat. Add chicken, prosciutto side down; cook 4 minutes. Turn chicken over and cook just until cooked through, about 3 minutes. Transfer to platter and cover to keep warm; reserve skillet.

Whisk wine with remaining 2 teaspoons flour in small bowl. Add broth and lemon juice to same skillet; bring to boil. Add wine mixture; whisk until sauce thickens slightly, about 30 seconds. Season to taste with salt and pepper. Spoon sauce over chicken and serve.

4 SERVINGS

Saltimbocca, an Italian classic, traditionally calls for veal—but tastes even better with chicken. Serve with a side of buttered orzo and a simple green salad, and uncork a bottle of Pinot Grigio.

Grilled Chicken Breasts with Tomato, Olive, and Feta Relish

- 1½ cups coarsely chopped cherry tomatoes (about 10 ounces)
- ½ cup pitted Kalamata olives, chopped
- 3 tablespoons extra-virgin olive oil, divided
- 2 tablespoons chopped fresh mint
- 1 tablespoon red wine vinegar
- ¾ cup crumbled feta cheese (about 3½ ounces)
- 4 large skinless boneless chicken breast halves (about 6 to 7 ounces each)

Mix cherry tomatoes, olives, 2 tablespoons oil, mint, and vinegar in medium bowl. Gently stir in cheese. Season relish with salt and pepper.

Prepare barbecue (medium-high heat). Brush chicken on both sides with remaining 1 tablespoon olive oil; sprinkle with salt and pepper. Grill chicken just until cooked through, about 7 minutes per side. Transfer chicken to plates and slice, if desired. Top with relish and serve.

4 SERVINGS

Chicken and Artichoke Fricassee with Morel Mushrooms

1½ lemons
12 baby artichokes

6 cups water
2 tablespoons all purpose flour plus additional for dredging
2 teaspoons salt
1 bay leaf

2 tablespoons butter
1 tablespoon olive oil
4 chicken thighs
4 chicken drumsticks
4 ounces fresh morel mushrooms
2 medium carrots, peeled, thinly sliced
2 large shallots, thinly sliced
2 tablespoons chopped fresh thyme, divided
1 garlic clove, minced
¼ cup dry white wine
½ cup low-salt chicken broth
¼ cup crème fraîche

Fill large bowl with water. Squeeze juice from 1 lemon into water; add lemon halves. Tear outer leaves from 1 artichoke until only pale green leaves remain. Cut top ¾ inch from top; trim end of stem. Cut in half lengthwise. Rub cut sides of artichoke with lemon half; transfer to bowl with lemon water. Repeat with remaining artichokes.

Bring 6 cups water, 2 tablespoons flour, 2 teaspoons salt, and bay leaf to boil in large saucepan. Add artichoke halves and cook until just tender, about 5 minutes. Drain.

Melt butter with oil in heavy large deep skillet over medium heat. Sprinkle chicken with salt and pepper. Dredge chicken in flour, shaking off excess. Cook chicken until golden brown, about 4 minutes per side. Transfer chicken to plate. Add mushrooms, carrots, and shallots to skillet. Sprinkle with salt and pepper. Sauté until vegetables begin to soften, about 4 minutes. Add 1 tablespoon thyme and garlic; sauté 1 minute. Add wine; bring to boil. Add broth and artichokes; bring to boil. Return chicken to skillet, reduce heat to medium low, cover, and simmer 20 minutes. Turn chicken, cover, and simmer until cooked through, about 15 minutes longer. Transfer chicken and vegetables to platter. Whisk crème fraîche into sauce in skillet; bring to boil. Season with salt and pepper. Pour sauce over chicken, sprinkle with remaining 1 tablespoon thyme, and serve.

4 TO 6 SERVINGS

Open-Face Turkey Burgers with Gruyère and Mushrooms

- 10 ounces ground turkey
- 3 tablespoons olive oil, divided
- 1/2 teaspoon (scant) salt
- 1/4 teaspoon ground black pepper
- 2 slices country-style bread, toasted
- Mayonnaise

- 8 ounces mushrooms, sliced
- 2 shallots, sliced
- 1 large garlic clove, chopped
- 2 thin slices Gruyère cheese

- 1 teaspoon white wine vinegar
- 1 cup thinly sliced arugula

Mix turkey, 1 teaspoon oil, salt, and pepper in medium bowl. Shape into two 1/2-inch-thick patties. Place 1 toasted bread slice on each of 2 plates; spread each with mayonnaise.

Heat 2 tablespoons oil in large nonstick skillet over medium-high heat. Add mushrooms, shallots, and garlic; sauté 2 minutes, then push to side of skillet. Add turkey patties to other side of skillet. Cook until brown on bottom, about 4 minutes. Turn patties over; top with cheese. Cook until patties are cooked through, cheese melts, and mushrooms are brown, stirring mushrooms often, about 4 minutes. Season mushrooms with salt and pepper.

Meanwhile, whisk vinegar and 2 teaspoons oil in small bowl; mix in arugula. Sprinkle with salt and pepper.

Spoon mushrooms onto bread; top with patties and arugula salad.

MAKES 2

Roasted Game Hens with Caramelized Root Vegetables and Dried-Currant Sauce

- 3 tablespoons butter
- 2 tablespoons extra-virgin olive oil
- 1 large onion, coarsely chopped (about 2 1/2 cups)
- 2 medium rutabagas, peeled, cut into 1/3-inch cubes (about 3 cups)
- 2 medium turnips, peeled, cut into 1/3-inch cubes (about 2 1/2 cups)
- 2 large carrots, peeled, cut into 1/3-inch cubes (about 2 cups)
- 2 large parsnips, peeled, cut into 1/3-inch cubes (about 1 1/2 cups)
- 2 1/2 cups diced celery (about 4 stalks)
- 2 7.25-ounce jars whole roasted peeled chestnuts, halved

6 garlic cloves, minced
2 tablespoons chopped fresh thyme

1/4 cup plus 1 tablespoon chopped fresh thyme
1/4 cup chopped shallots
1/4 cup extra-virgin olive oil
1 1/2 tablespoons finely grated orange peel
4 garlic cloves, minced
1 tablespoon juniper berries,* crushed in mortar with pestle
3 1 3/4-pound Cornish game hens, thawed if frozen, cut lengthwise in half, rinsed, patted dry

1 1/2 cups low-salt chicken broth

1/4 cup dried currants

This delicious one-dish meal is really nice with an India pale ale, or you can pour a French Chablis.

Melt butter with oil in very large pot over medium-high heat. Add onion; sauté 5 minutes. Add rutabagas and next 4 ingredients; sauté until caramelized and tender, stirring often, about 30 minutes. Stir in chestnuts, garlic, and thyme; sauté 5 minutes. Season generously with salt and pepper. *(Can be made 1 day ahead. Cover and chill. Rewarm over medium heat, stirring often, until heated through before serving.)*

Mix 1/4 cup thyme, shallots, oil, orange peel, garlic, and crushed juniper berries in small bowl for marinade. Rub all over hens. Place in large roasting pan; cover and chill at least 6 hours or overnight.

Preheat oven to 325°F. Pour 1 1/2 cups broth into roasting pan with hens. Sprinkle hens with salt and pepper. Cover pan tightly with foil. Roast until hens are cooked through and juices run clear when thighs are pierced with fork, about 1 hour 15 minutes. Remove from oven. Preheat broiler.

Pour pan juices from hens into small saucepan; add dried currants and 1 tablespoon thyme. Boil until liquid is reduced to 1 cup, about 5 minutes (sauce will be thin). Season with salt and pepper.

Meanwhile, broil hens until lightly browned, watching closely to avoid burning, about 4 minutes. Place 1 hen half on each plate. Divide caramelized vegetables among plates. Spoon sauce over hens and serve immediately.

**Available in the spice section of most supermarkets.*

6 SERVINGS

Spice-Rubbed Duck Legs Braised with Green Olives and Carrots

- 1 tablespoon coriander seeds
- 1 teaspoon fennel seeds
- 1 teaspoon cumin seeds
- ½ teaspoon whole black peppercorns
- 4 teaspoons coarse kosher salt
- 6 whole duck leg-thigh pieces (about 7¾ pounds), trimmed of excess skin and fat

- ¼ cup brandy
- 1 cup dry white wine
- 1½ cups low-salt chicken broth
- 2 medium onions, halved, cut into ½-inch-thick wedges
- 6 garlic cloves, peeled
- 3 3x½-inch strips lemon peel (yellow part only)
- 2 bay leaves
- 3 carrots, peeled, halved lengthwise, cut crosswise into 1-inch pieces
- 1 cup picholine olives* or other brine-cured green olives

- 2 teaspoons honey (optional)

Toast first 4 ingredients in medium skillet over medium heat until fragrant, about 2 minutes. Transfer to mortar or spice grinder; grind to coarse powder. Transfer to small bowl; stir in salt. Arrange duck legs on rimmed baking sheet; sprinkle spice mixture over all sides. Refrigerate uncovered overnight.

Preheat oven to 300°F. Pat duck gently to remove moisture, removing as little spice mixture as possible. Heat heavy large skillet over medium-high heat. Working in batches, cook duck, skin side down, until skin is crisp and brown, about 7 minutes. Turn duck legs and cook until brown, about 3 minutes longer, draining fat from skillet between batches. Transfer duck legs to roasting pan, skin side up. Pour fat from skillet. Remove skillet from heat; add brandy. Bring to boil over medium-high heat, scraping up browned bits. Add wine. Boil until liquid is reduced by half, about 3 minutes. Add broth; bring to boil. Pour mixture over duck in pan. Tuck onion wedges, garlic cloves, lemon peel, and bay leaves between duck legs. Scatter carrots and olives over. Cover with foil.

Braise duck in oven 1 hour. Turn legs over; allow vegetables to fall into broth. Cover; braise until duck is tender and meat is falling from bones, about 1 hour longer. *(Can be made 1 day ahead. Cool slightly. Cover and chill. Rewarm in 350°F oven 20 minutes.)*

Preheat broiler. Transfer duck, skin-side up, to rimmed baking sheet. Tent with foil. Transfer vegetables and olives from sauce to bowl; cover to keep warm. Spoon fat from sauce in roasting pan. Transfer remaining sauce to large skillet. Simmer sauce over medium-high heat until reduced to 1 cup, about 10 minutes. Season with salt and pepper, and honey, if desired. Keep warm.

Meanwhile, place duck legs under broiler until skin is crisp, about 4 minutes, watching carefully to prevent burning. Transfer to serving platter, spoon vegetable mixture around duck legs, drizzle sauce over, and serve immediately.

**A medium-size, firm, brine-cured green olive; sold at the deli counter of some supermarkets and at specialty foods stores.*

6 SERVINGS

The duck marinates overnight in a spice rub, so start this recipe one day ahead.

Crunchy Wasabi Salmon with Lime

- 3/4 cup wasabi peas (about 3 ounces)
- 4 8-ounce salmon fillets with skin (each about 1 inch to 1 1/4 inches thick)
- 1 tablespoon finely grated lime peel
- 2 tablespoons olive oil, divided

- 6 cups thinly sliced red cabbage (about 1/2 large head)
- 1 8-ounce package trimmed sugar snap peas

- 2 tablespoons fresh lime juice
- Lime wedges

Preheat oven to 400°F. Blend wasabi peas in processor until ground but with some coarsely crushed pieces. Lightly oil rimmed baking sheet. Arrange salmon fillets, skin side down, on prepared baking sheet. Sprinkle fish with salt. Press ground wasabi peas onto tops of salmon fillets to adhere, covering tops completely. Sprinkle grated lime peel over salmon; drizzle with 1 tablespoon oil. Roast salmon just until opaque in center, about 10 minutes.

Meanwhile, heat remaining 1 tablespoon oil in large nonstick skillet over medium-high heat. Add cabbage and sugar snap peas; sauté until vegetables are crisp-tender, about 5 minutes. Season to taste with salt and pepper.

Transfer 1 salmon fillet to each of 4 plates. Drizzle with lime juice. Mound cabbage-snap pea mixture alongside. Garnish with lime wedges and serve.

4 SERVINGS

Wasabi peas are dried green peas that are covered in a spicy coating made from wasabi powder. They can be found at some supermarkets and natural foods stores, and at Asian markets. Serve the salmon with a bowl of steamed jasmine rice and a bottle of Riesling.

Halibut in Chard Leaves with Lemon-Thyme Butter

- ½ cup (1 stick) butter, room temperature
- 1 tablespoon fresh lemon juice
- 1 tablespoon chopped fresh thyme
- 1 tablespoon chopped fresh chives
- 2 teaspoons grated lemon peel
- 4 very large Swiss chard leaves, halved lengthwise, center stems cut out
- 4 1-inch-thick halibut fillets (each 6 to 8 ounces)
- 4 lemon slices

Preheat oven to 450°F. Blend butter, fresh lemon juice, chopped fresh thyme, chopped fresh chives, and grated lemon peel in small bowl; season butter to taste with salt and pepper.

Place four 12-inch squares of foil on work surface. Overlap center edge of 2 chard halves on each square. Sprinkle fillets on each side with salt and pepper, then spread with some lemon-thyme butter. Top each with lemon slice. Place 1 fillet crosswise on widest part of chard. Fold bottom of leaf over fillet, then continue to roll up (sides will be open). Enclose each wrapped fillet in foil.

Arrange packets on rimmed baking sheet. Bake until fish is just opaque in center, 12 to 14 minutes. Transfer packets to plates, open foil, and serve.

4 SERVINGS

For a lighter version of this dish, wrap the fish in very large butter lettuce leaves.

Tuna Kebabs with Ginger-Chile Marinade

3 tablespoons unseasoned rice vinegar
2 tablespoons finely grated peeled fresh ginger
2 tablespoons peanut oil
2 tablespoons Asian sesame oil
2 tablespoons soy sauce
2 tablespoons honey
1 tablespoon chopped fresh cilantro
1 serrano chile, seeded, minced
Freshly ground white pepper
1½ pounds 1¼-inch-thick ahi tuna, cut into 1- to 1¼-inch cubes

Nonstick vegetable oil spray
1 large red bell pepper, cut into 1-inch squares
1 large sweet onion (such as Maui or Vidalia), cut into 1-inch squares
6 12-inch-long metal skewers
Additional chopped fresh cilantro

Whisk first 8 ingredients in medium bowl to blend; season to taste with ground white pepper. Transfer 3 tablespoons marinade to small bowl and reserve. Add tuna to remaining marinade in medium bowl and toss to coat. Refrigerate at least 30 minutes and up to 45 minutes.

Spray grill rack with nonstick spray. Prepare barbecue (medium-high heat). Alternate tuna cubes, bell pepper squares, and onion squares on each of 6 metal skewers. Grill to desired doneness, turning frequently, about 4 minutes total for medium-rare. Transfer to platter. Drizzle reserved marinade over; sprinkle with chopped cilantro.

4 SERVINGS

Fish and Chips with Tarragon-Malt Vinegar Mayonnaise

- 3/4 cup mayonnaise
- 3 tablespoons chopped fresh tarragon
- 1 tablespoon malt vinegar or cider vinegar

- 1 cup self-rising flour
- 1 1/2 teaspoons Old Bay seasoning
- 1 1/4 cups lager beer
- Vegetable oil (for frying)
- 1 1/2 pounds halibut fillets, cut crosswise into 1/2- to 3/4-inch-thick slices
- 3 8- to 10-ounce red-skinned potatoes or russet potatoes, unpeeled, cut into 1/8- to 1/4-inch-thick rounds

Whisk mayonnaise, tarragon, and vinegar in small bowl to blend. Season to taste with salt and pepper.

Whisk flour and Old Bay seasoning in medium bowl to blend. Add beer and whisk just until blended. Pour enough oil into heavy large skillet to reach depth of 1 inch; heat oil to 350°F. Sprinkle fish with salt and pepper. Working in batches, dip fish into beer batter to coat lightly, allowing excess batter to drip back into bowl. Add fish to hot oil and fry until deep golden and just cooked through, about 3 minutes per side. Transfer fish to paper towels to drain. Working in batches, add potato slices to oil and cook until golden and tender, turning occasionally, about 4 minutes. Transfer to paper towels to drain. Sprinkle generously with salt.

Divide fish and chips among 4 plates. Spoon tarragon-malt vinegar mayonnaise alongside and serve.

4 SERVINGS

Pacific Rim Dinner for 8

Assorted Sushi

Cold Sake

Tuna Kebabs with Ginger-Chile Marinade
(double recipe; opposite; pictured opposite)

Baby Bok Choy with Braised Shiitake Sauce
(page 140)

Jasmine Rice with Garlic, Ginger, and Cilantro
(page 143)

Riesling

Mango Sorbet

Almond Cookies

Tea

Soy-Marinated Fish

FISH

1½ pounds ¾-inch-thick hake or pollack fillets, cut into 2x3- or 2x4-inch pieces
½ cup chopped green onions
3 tablespoons minced peeled fresh ginger
3 tablespoons Shaoxing wine (Chinese rice wine)* or dry Sherry, divided
2 tablespoons peanut oil or vegetable oil, divided
1 tablespoon soy sauce

SAUCE

3 tablespoons sugar
2 tablespoons soy sauce
2 tablespoons Asian sesame oil
2 tablespoons Shaoxing wine (Chinese rice wine) or dry Sherry
1 tablespoon dark soy sauce*
1 whole star anise*

¼ cup chopped green onions

FOR FISH: Rinse fish and pat dry. Mix green onions, ginger, 1 tablespoon rice wine, 1 tablespoon oil, and soy sauce in 11x7x2-inch glass baking dish. Add fish and turn to coat. Let marinate 1 hour at room temperature.

FOR SAUCE: Bring first 6 ingredients to boil in heavy small saucepan, stirring to dissolve sugar. Reduce heat to medium and simmer until sauce is slightly thickened and reduced to ⅓ cup, about 4 minutes. Remove star anise sauce from heat and cool.

Remove fish from marinade and place on several layers of paper towels to drain; reserve marinade. Pat fish dry. Heat 14-inch-diameter flat-bottomed wok over high heat until drop of water added to wok evaporates on contact. Add remaining 1 tablespoon oil to wok, then fish pieces, spreading evenly. Cover and cook 30 seconds. Uncover and loosen fish pieces with metal spatula. Reduce heat to medium and cook 1 minute. Turn fish pieces over; cook 1 minute. Add remaining 2 tablespoons rice wine and reserved marinade from fish. Cover and cook 1 minute. Remove wok from heat; let fish stand, covered, until just opaque in center, about 1 minute. Using metal spatula, transfer fish and sauce from wok to plate. Drizzle with some of star anise sauce. Refrigerate until cold. *(Can be made 6 hours ahead. Cover fish and keep chilled. Cover remaining star anise sauce and let stand at room temperature.)*

Spoon additional star anise sauce over fish; sprinkle with green onions and serve cold or at room temperature.

**Available at Asian markets.*

4 SERVINGS

Grilled Halibut with Basil-Shallot Butter

1½ cups (loosely packed) fresh basil leaves
1 large shallot, coarsely chopped
8 tablespoons (½ cup) unsalted butter, room temperature
1 teaspoon grated lemon peel

6 6-ounce halibut fillets
Extra-virgin olive oil

Finely chop basil and shallot in mini food processor. Add butter, 2 tablespoons at a time, and process until blended, stopping occasionally to scrape down sides. Transfer to small bowl; stir in lemon peel. Season basil-shallot butter with salt.

Prepare barbecue (medium heat). Rub fish fillets on both sides with olive oil. Grill until fillets are just opaque in center, about 4 minutes per side. Transfer fish to plates. Immediately spread some basil-shallot butter over fish. Serve, passing additional basil-shallot butter alongside.

6 SERVINGS

Salmon with Pineapple Salsa and Spicy Chile Sauce

Canned chipotle chiles can be found in the Latin foods section of most supermarkets.

- 1/4 cup mayonnaise
- 1 1/4 teaspoons chopped canned chipotle chiles in adobo sauce
- 1 cup diced cored fresh pineapple
- 2 tablespoons ginger preserves or orange marmalade
- 1 tablespoon fresh lime juice
- 1 teaspoon minced peeled fresh ginger
- 2 tablespoons chopped fresh cilantro

- 4 6-ounce salmon fillets with skin (each 1 to 1 1/4 inches thick)
- 2 tablespoons olive oil

Mix mayonnaise and chipotle chiles in small bowl. Mix pineapple, ginger preserves, lime juice, fresh ginger, and cilantro in another small bowl for salsa. Season salsa with salt and pepper.

Brush salmon with oil; sprinkle with salt and pepper. Heat heavy large skillet over medium-high heat. Add salmon and sauté until just opaque in center, about 5 minutes per side. Transfer fish to plates. Spoon chile mayonnaise over. Spoon pineapple salsa alongside.

4 SERVINGS

Fennel- and Coriander-Spiced Salmon Fillets

There are only four ingredients in this dish, yet it is packed with flavor. Serve it with a crisp, dry rosé.

- 1 1/2 tablespoons fennel seeds
- 1 1/2 teaspoons coriander seeds
- 6 6-ounce skinless salmon fillets (each about 1 to 1 1/4 inches thick)
- Extra-virgin olive oil

Prepare barbecue (high heat). Coarsely grind fennel seeds and coriander seeds in spice grinder. Brush salmon fillets generously with oil. Sprinkle both sides of fillets with salt and pepper, then with spice mixture, pressing to adhere. Grill salmon, covered, until center is just opaque, about 4 minutes per side.

6 SERVINGS

Striped Bass with Saffron Vegetables and Spiced Broccoli Rabe

SAFFRON BUTTER

- 1½ teaspoons fennel seeds
- ½ teaspoon aniseed
- ½ teaspoon whole white peppercorns
- ½ teaspoon minced fresh thyme
- ¼ teaspoon (scant) saffron threads
- ½ cup (1 stick) butter, room temperature
- 1½ teaspoons tomato paste

SPICED BROCCOLI RABE

- 3 garlic cloves, unpeeled
- 1 teaspoon plus 2 tablespoons olive oil

- ¼ cup coarsely chopped pitted picholine olives* or other brine-cured green olives
- 2 tablespoons drained capers
- 2 tablespoons raisins
- 4 anchovy fillets, rinsed
- ½ teaspoon dried crushed red pepper

- 1 bunch broccoli rabe (rapini; about 1 pound), cut crosswise into ½-inch slices

VEGETABLES AND FISH

- 1½ cups chicken broth
- 1 large head of cauliflower, cut into small florets
- 2 medium-size yellow squash, cut into ½-inch cubes
- 1½ cups sliced radishes

- 6 6-ounce farmed striped bass fillets with skin
- All purpose flour (for dredging)
- 2 tablespoons vegetable oil

FOR SAFFRON BUTTER: Finely grind first 5 ingredients in spice grinder. Transfer to small bowl. Add butter and tomato paste; stir to blend. Season with salt and pepper. *(Can be made 2 days ahead. Cover and chill.)*

FOR SPICED BROCCOLI RABE: Preheat oven to 350°F. Place garlic in small ovenproof dish. Drizzle with 1 teaspoon oil, cover tightly with foil, and roast until tender, about 30 minutes. Cool; peel.

Place roasted garlic, remaining 2 tablespoons oil, olives, capers, raisins, anchovies, and crushed red pepper in mortar. Mash with pestle or process in mini processor until coarse puree forms. *(Spiced puree can be made 1 day ahead. Transfer to small bowl and chill.)*

Cook broccoli rabe in large saucepan of boiling salted water until stems are crisp-tender,

about 5 minutes. Drain, pressing on broccoli rabe to release excess water. Transfer to medium bowl. Add spiced puree and toss to coat. *(Can be made 2 hours ahead. Let stand at room temperature.)*

FOR VEGETABLES AND FISH: Bring broth to boil in heavy large saucepan. Add cauliflower, squash, and radishes. Sprinkle with salt and pepper. Cover and simmer 3 minutes. Uncover, add 6 tablespoons saffron butter, and simmer until vegetables are tender and broth thickens slightly, stirring frequently, about 4 minutes.

Meanwhile, sprinkle fish with salt and pepper, then dredge in flour. Heat 1 tablespoon oil in each of 2 large skillets over medium-high heat. Place 3 fillets, skin side down, in each skillet and cook until brown, about 3 minutes per side.

Divide vegetables and broth among 6 shallow soup bowls. Top each with fish fillet, skin side up. Top with spiced broccoli rabe and serve.

American farmed striped bass is raised in contained ponds with circulating water; it's a safer choice than wild striped bass, which is high in mercury.

**Medium-size, firm, brine-cured green olives; sold at the deli counter of some supermarkets and at specialty foods stores.* ∆

6 SERVINGS

Mixed Seafood Grill with Paprika-Lemon Dressing

7 tablespoons olive oil, divided
1/4 cup fresh lemon juice plus lemon wedges for garnish
2 tablespoons chopped fresh Italian parsley
3 garlic cloves, thinly sliced
2 teaspoons paprika

Nonstick vegetable oil spray
2 pounds 1-inch-thick firm white fish fillets (such as halibut), cut crosswise into 2-inch-wide strips
2 pounds uncooked large shrimp, peeled, deveined, tails left intact
2 pounds cleaned fresh or thawed frozen squid, each body cut open on 1 long side and scored lightly (tentacles reserved for another use)

Whisk 4 tablespoons oil, lemon juice, parsley, garlic, and paprika in small bowl. Season with salt and pepper. *(Cover and chill up to 6 hours. Bring to room temperature before using.)*

Spray grill rack with nonstick spray. Prepare barbecue (medium-high heat). Arrange seafood on baking sheets. Drizzle with 3 tablespoons oil and turn to coat; sprinkle with salt and pepper. Transfer seafood to grill. Cook until just opaque in center, about 4 minutes per side for fish, 2 minutes per side for shrimp, and 30 seconds per side for squid. Arrange on platter. Spoon dressing over. Garnish with lemon wedges.

6 SERVINGS

Shrimp and Andouille Sausage with Creole Mustard Sauce

1 pound uncooked peeled deveined large shrimp
1 tablespoon Creole or Cajun seasoning*
2 tablespoons vegetable oil, divided
1 pound andouille sausage, cut crosswise on diagonal into ¾-inch-thick pieces
1 large onion, halved, thinly sliced
1 large red bell pepper, cut into ⅓-inch-wide strips
1 tablespoon chopped fresh thyme
1 cup low-salt chicken broth
5 tablespoons Creole mustard (such as Zatarain's)
2 teaspoons red wine vinegar

Toss shrimp with Creole seasoning in medium bowl to coat. Heat 1 tablespoon oil in heavy large skillet over high heat. Add sausage pieces, cut side down. Cook until browned on both sides, about 5 minutes. Transfer sausage to bowl. Add shrimp to skillet; cook until browned and just opaque in center, about 3 minutes. Transfer to bowl with sausage. Add 1 tablespoon oil, onion, bell pepper, and thyme to skillet. Sauté until vegetables are beginning to soften, about 5 minutes. Add broth, mustard, and vinegar. Stir until sauce thickens, about 2 minutes. Return sausage and shrimp to skillet. Simmer until heated through, stirring occasionally, about 1 minute. Season with salt and pepper.

**Available in the spice section of most supermarkets.* Δ

4 TO 6 SERVINGS

Dinner from the Grill for 6

Prosciuitto and Fig Bruschetta
(page 18)

Mixed Seafood Grill with Paprika-Lemon Dressing
(opposite; pictured opposite)

Green Bean, Orange, and Green Olive Salad
(page 157)

Grilled Flatbreads with Za'atar
(page 167)

Sauvignon Blanc

Gilled Peaches with Fresh Raspberry Sauce
(page 193)

Cauliflower and Caramelized Onion Tart

- 1 small head of cauliflower (about 1 pound), cored, cut into 1-inch florets
- 2½ tablespoons olive oil, divided
- 1 tablespoon truffle oil*
- 1 refrigerated pie crust
- 1 large onion, halved lengthwise, thinly sliced
- 1 tablespoon Dijon mustard
- 2 large eggs
- 1 7- to 8-ounce container mascarpone cheese (Italian cream cheese)*
- ½ cup whipping cream
- ¼ teaspoon ground white pepper
- Pinch of ground nutmeg
- 1 cup grated Gruyère cheese
- ¾ cup grated Parmesan cheese

MEATLESS

Position rack in center of oven; preheat to 425°F. Toss cauliflower with 1 tablespoon oil in large bowl. Spread on rimmed baking sheet, spacing apart. Sprinkle with salt and pepper. Roast 15 minutes; turn florets over. Continue roasting until tender, about 25 minutes longer. Cool cauliflower; slice thinly. Drizzle with truffle oil; toss. Reduce oven temperature to 350°F.

Press pie crust onto bottom and up sides of 9-inch-diameter tart pan with removable bottom. Line pie crust with foil; fill with pie weights. Bake crust 20 minutes. Remove foil and pie weights; bake until crust is golden, about 5 minutes, pressing crust with back of fork if bubbles form. Cool crust. Maintain oven temperature.

Heat remaining 1½ tablespoons olive oil in heavy large skillet over medium heat. Add onion; sprinkle with salt and pepper. Cook until onion is deep golden brown, stirring occasionally, about 40 minutes. Cool slightly. *(Can be made 1 day ahead. Store crust at room temperature. Cover and chill cauliflower and onion separately.)*

Brush bottom and sides of crust with mustard. Spread onion in crust. Arrange cauliflower evenly over. Set tart on rimmed baking sheet. Whisk eggs and next 4 ingredients in medium bowl. Stir in Gruyère. Pour mixture over filling in tart pan; sprinkle with Parmesan. Bake until tart is golden and center is set, about 40 minutes. Transfer to rack; cool 15 minutes before serving.

**Available at some supermarkets, specialty foods stores, and Italian markets.*

8 SERVINGS

Great with orange or Romanesco cauliflower. Serve with a green salad and Chardonnay.

Grab-and-Go Greek Sandwiches

Tapenade can be found near the olives at the market.

- 2 tablespoons olive oil
- 1 tablespoon fresh lemon juice
- 2 cups (packed) torn romaine lettuce
- 1 cup drained garbanzo beans (chickpeas)
- 1 cup diced feta cheese
- 1 tomato, cored, cut into thin wedges
- ½ cup thinly sliced red onion

- 2 7-inch-diameter pita breads, cut in half to make 4 semicircles

- Purchased tapenade (olive paste)

Whisk oil and lemon juice in large bowl; season with salt and pepper. Add lettuce, garbanzo beans, cheese, tomato, and onion; toss to coat. Using tongs, turn pitas over gas flame or in broiler to char slightly, about 15 seconds per side. Pull each open, spread with tapenade, and fill with salad.

2 SERVINGS

Eggplant and Green Bean Curry with Ginger and Cilantro

5 tablespoons vegetable oil, divided
4 garlic cloves, chopped
1 tablespoon chopped peeled fresh ginger
1 14- to 16-ounce eggplant, peeled, cut into 2x½x½-inch sticks
8 ounces green beans, trimmed, cut into 2-inch pieces
1 tablespoon grated lime peel
1 teaspoon Thai green curry paste*
1 cup canned unsweetened coconut milk*
3 green onions, chopped
¼ cup chopped fresh cilantro
2 tablespoons chopped fresh mint
Steamed rice

Heat 4 tablespoons oil in large skillet over medium-high heat. Add garlic and ginger; stir 30 seconds. Add eggplant and green beans. Cook until almost tender, stirring often, about 10 minutes. Cover and cook until completely tender, about 3 minutes longer. Transfer vegetables to bowl. Add 1 tablespoon oil, lime peel, and curry paste to same skillet; stir 15 seconds. Add coconut milk; bring to boil, whisking until smooth. Return vegetables to skillet; toss until sauce thickens enough to coat vegetables, about 3 minutes. Season with salt. Mix in onions, cilantro, and mint. Serve over steamed rice.

**Available in the Asian foods section of the supermarket.*

2 SERVINGS

Five-Spice Tofu Stir-Fry with Carrots and Celery

2 tablespoons peanut oil or vegetable oil, divided
8 ounces savory baked five-spice tofu cakes* (about 2 squares), cut into matchstick-size strips
2 cups matchstick-size strips carrots (about 3 medium)
2 cups matchstick-size strips celery (about 3 long stalks)
⅓ cup finely chopped rinsed canned Szechuan preserved vegetable* (about 1¼ ounces)
1 tablespoon Shaoxing wine (Chinese rice wine)* or dry Sherry
½ teaspoon salt
½ teaspoon sugar
¼ teaspoon ground white pepper
2 teaspoons Asian sesame oil

Heat 14-inch-diameter flat-bottomed wok or heavy 12-inch-diameter skillet over high heat until drop of water added to wok evaporates on contact. Add 1 tablespoon peanut oil and

swirl, then add tofu and stir-fry until tofu just begins to brown, about 1 minute. Transfer tofu to plate. Add remaining 1 tablespoon peanut oil to same wok (do not clean). Add carrots, celery, and Szechuan preserved vegetable and stir-fry until carrots are crisp-tender, about 3 minutes. Return tofu to wok; add rice wine, salt, sugar, and white pepper. Stir-fry to blend, about 1 minute. Remove pan from heat; stir in sesame oil and serve.

**Available at Asian markets.*

4 SERVINGS

Dinner in the Kitchen for 4

Miso Soup

Five-Spice Tofu Stir-Fry with Carrots and Celery
(opposite; pictured at left)

Steamed Rice

Gewürztraminer

Warm Doughnuts à la Mode with Bananas and Spiced Caramel Sauce
(double recipe; page 192)

Spanish-Style Grilled Vegetables with Breadcrumb Picada

Picada **is a Spanish flavoring made with garlic, herbs, and ground nuts. Here, breadcrumbs stand in for the nuts. Uncork a crisp white Tempranillo wine to go with the vegetables.**

- 3 large red bell peppers (about 1½ pounds), stemmed, seeded, quartered
- 4 large Japanese eggplants (about 1¼ pounds), trimmed, cut lengthwise into 3 slices
- 4 medium-size green or yellow zucchini (preferably 2 of each; about 1 pound), trimmed, cut lengthwise into ⅓-inch-thick slices
- Extra-virgin olive oil (for grilling)

- 6 tablespoons extra-virgin olive oil, divided
- 2 garlic cloves, finely chopped
- ½ teaspoon dried crushed red pepper
- ½ cup panko (Japanese breadcrumbs)*

- 2 tablespoons Sherry wine vinegar
- ¼ cup chopped fresh Italian parsley
- 2 tablespoons chopped fresh oregano

Prepare barbecue (medium heat). Arrange vegetables on baking sheets. Brush with oil; sprinkle with salt and pepper. Grill peppers, skin side down and without turning, until blackened and blistered, moving occasionally for even cooking, about 10 minutes. Enclose in plastic bag. Let stand until skins loosen, about 30 minutes. Grill eggplants and zucchini until charred and tender, turning and rearranging for even browning, 5 to 6 minutes. Place on foil-lined baking sheet. Peel peppers. Transfer to sheet with eggplants and zucchini.

Heat 3 tablespoons olive oil in medium skillet over medium heat. Add garlic and crushed red pepper; stir until fragrant, about 30 seconds. Add breadcrumbs; stir until golden, about 3 minutes. Season breadcrumb picada to taste with salt; scrape into small bowl.

Place vinegar in another small bowl; whisk in 3 tablespoons oil. Mix in parsley and oregano. Season to taste with salt.

Arrange vegetables on platter. Spoon herb dressing over; sprinkle with breadcrumbs.

**Sold in the Asian foods section of some supermarkets and at Asian markets.*

6 SERVINGS

Giant Southwestern Omelet

- 1 15- to 15½-ounce can black beans, rinsed, drained
- ¾ cup purchased tomatillo salsa

- 4 large eggs
- 2 green onions, chopped
- ¼ teaspoon salt
- ¼ teaspoon ground black pepper
- 3 tablespoons butter, divided
- ½ red bell pepper, cut into strips
- 2 cups sliced mushrooms (about 5 ounces)

- 1 cup (packed) coarsely grated Monterey Jack cheese (about 4 ounces)
- 3 tablespoons chopped fresh cilantro

Stir black beans and tomatillo salsa in heavy medium saucepan over medium heat until heated through. Remove bean and salsa mixture from heat. Cover and keep warm while preparing omelet.

Whisk eggs, onions, salt, and pepper in medium bowl to blend. Melt 2 tablespoons butter in medium nonstick skillet over medium heat. Add bell pepper and sliced mushrooms to skillet; stir until mushrooms are brown, about 8 minutes. Transfer to bowl.

Melt 1 tablespoon butter in same skillet over medium heat. Add egg mixture. Cook without stirring until beginning to set, about 4 minutes. Sprinkle with vegetables, cheese, and 1 tablespoon cilantro. Cover skillet and cook until cheese melts and eggs are set, about 2 minutes. Slide large spatula under omelet to loosen. Fold in half; turn out onto platter. Top with bean and salsa mixture. Sprinkle with 2 tablespoons cilantro and serve.

2 SERVINGS

Israeli Couscous Risotto with Squash, Radicchio, and Parsley Butter

- 6 tablespoons (¾ stick) butter, room temperature, divided
- 1 large onion, chopped (2½ cups)
- 3 teaspoons grated lemon peel, divided
- 1 8.8-ounce package toasted Israeli couscous (about 1¾ cups)
- 3 cups low-salt vegetable broth
- 3 cups ½-inch cubes peeled butternut squash (about 12 ounces)
- 1 cup diced radicchio
- ¾ cup finely grated Parmesan cheese

- 1 cup (packed) fresh Italian parsley leaves

Melt 2 tablespoons butter in heavy large saucepan over medium-high heat. Add onion and 2 teaspoons lemon peel. Cover and cook 5 minutes. Add couscous; sauté 2 minutes. Add broth and squash; bring to boil. Reduce heat to medium. Cook, uncovered, until couscous and squash are tender and mixture is still moist, about 10 minutes. Mix in radicchio and cheese. Season to taste with salt and pepper.

Meanwhile, finely chop parsley in mini processor. Add 4 tablespoons butter and 1 teaspoon lemon peel; blend well. Season to taste with salt and pepper.

Transfer couscous to bowl. Swirl half of parsley butter into top of couscous. Serve, passing remaining parsley butter.

4 TO 6 SERVINGS

Israeli couscous, which is larger and chewier than the more common variety, takes the place of arborio rice in this risotto-style dish. Find it in the pasta section of many supermarkets or at Middle Eastern markets.

Mustard-Crusted Tofu with Kale and Sweet Potato

- 1 14-ounce package firm tofu
- ½ cup whole grain Dijon mustard

- 4 tablespoons vegetable oil, divided
- ½ medium onion, sliced
- 1 tablespoon minced peeled fresh ginger
- 1 bunch kale, stem cut from each leaf, leaves thinly sliced crosswise (about 8 cups)
- 1 small red-skinned sweet potato (yam; about 8 ounces), peeled, halved lengthwise, thinly sliced crosswise
- 2 tablespoons fresh lime juice

Cut tofu into eight ½-inch-thick slices. Arrange on paper towels; drain 10 minutes. Spread both sides of each slice with mustard.

Heat 2 tablespoons oil in large nonstick skillet over medium-high heat. Add onion and ginger; sauté 1 minute. Add kale, sweet potato, and lime juice. Cover, reduce heat to low, and cook until potato is tender and kale is wilted, about 12 minutes.

Meanwhile, heat remaining 2 tablespoons oil in another large nonstick skillet over medium heat. Add tofu; cover and cook until heated through and crisp, about 2 minutes per side (some mustard seeds may fall off tofu).

Arrange kale and sweet potato mixture on plate. Overlap tofu slices atop vegetables and serve.

4 SERVINGS

Mushroom and Caper Frittata

- 4 large eggs
- 4 tablespoons freshly grated Parmesan cheese, divided
- 2 tablespoons chopped fresh basil
- 1 tablespoon chopped fresh oregano
- 1 teaspoon Dijon mustard
- 1/4 teaspoon ground black pepper
- ≥1/8 teaspoon salt

- 2 tablespoons olive oil
- 3 baby portobello mushrooms, stemmed, caps thickly sliced
- 4 teaspoons drained capers

Preheat broiler. Whisk eggs, 2 tablespoons Parmesan cheese, basil, oregano, Dijon mustard, pepper, and salt in medium bowl to blend.

Heat oil in small ovenproof skillet over medium-high heat. Add mushrooms and capers. Sauté until mushrooms are brown and juices evaporate, about 6 minutes. Pour in egg mixture. Reduce heat to low. Cook without stirring until eggs are almost set, about 4 minutes. Sprinkle with remaining 2 tablespoons cheese. Broil until top is brown and set, about 1 minute.

Cool frittata 5 minutes. Run spatula around edges to loosen and slide out onto plate. Cut in half and serve.

2 SERVINGS

Post-Hike Lunch for 4

Watermelon-Lime Agua Fresca
(page 38)

Mushroom and Caper Frittata
(double recipe; at left)

Mixed Green Salad

Iced Tea and *Sparkling Water*

Chocolate-Caramel Slice
(page 226)

Spicy Spinach Linguine with Olive Oil and Garlic

- 12 ounces spinach linguine

- 6 tablespoons extra-virgin olive oil
- 1 cup chopped fresh basil, divided
- 4 garlic cloves, minced
- ½ teaspoon dried crushed red pepper
- ½ cup dry white wine
- 1½ cups grated Pecorino Romano cheese, divided

Cook linguine in large pot of boiling salted water until just tender but still firm to bite. Drain, reserving 1 cup pasta cooking liquid. Return pasta to same pot.

Meanwhile, heat oil in heavy large skillet over medium-high heat. Add ½ cup basil, garlic, and red pepper; stir 1 minute. Add wine and boil until slightly reduced, about 3 minutes. Add mixture from skillet, remaining ½ cup basil, and ¾ cup cheese to pasta. Toss over medium heat until sauce coats pasta, adding reserved pasta liquid by ¼ cupfuls if dry. Season with salt and pepper. Transfer to bowl. Sprinkle with remaining ¾ cup cheese.

2 TO 4 SERVINGS

Penne with Grilled Eggplant and Radicchio Sauce

- 2 small eggplants (about 1½ pounds total)

- 1 large head of radicchio (about 8 ounces), quartered, cored
- 7 tablespoons olive oil, divided

- ⅓ cup finely chopped onion
- 3 garlic cloves, thinly sliced
- 2 tablespoons fresh Italian parsley leaves
- 1 tablespoon chopped fresh thyme
- 1 cup chopped seeded peeled tomatoes
- ½ cup low-salt chicken broth
- ⅓ cup dry white wine
- ½ cup coarsely chopped fresh basil
- ¼ teaspoon dried crushed red pepper

- 12 ounces penne or fusilli (spiral-shaped pasta), freshly cooked
- 6 ounces soft fresh goat cheese, crumbled

Cut eggplants in half lengthwise, then cut crosswise into ½-inch-thick slices. Place on layers of paper towels. Sprinkle eggplant lightly with salt; let stand 30 minutes.

Prepare barbecue (medium-high heat). Pat eggplant dry. Brush eggplant and radicchio with 3 tablespoons oil; sprinkle with salt. Grill until eggplant is tender and radicchio is wilted, about 4 minutes per side for eggplant and 1 minute per side for radicchio. Transfer radicchio to cutting board; chop coarsely.

Heat 3 tablespoons oil in heavy large skillet over medium heat. Add onion and garlic; stir 2 minutes. Add parsley and thyme. Reduce heat to low; sauté until onion is soft, about 10 minutes. Add next 5 ingredients; simmer 8 minutes, stirring frequently. Stir in eggplant and radicchio. Season to taste with salt and pepper.

Toss pasta with 1 tablespoon oil in large bowl. Add eggplant sauce and toss. Sprinkle with crumbled goat cheese; serve.

6 SERVINGS

Spicy Sesame Noodles with Chopped Peanuts and Thai Basil

- 1 tablespoon peanut oil
- 2 tablespoons minced peeled fresh ginger
- 2 garlic cloves, minced
- 3 tablespoons Asian sesame oil
- 2 tablespoons soy sauce
- 2 tablespoons balsamic vinegar
- 1½ tablespoons sugar
- 1 tablespoon (or more) hot chili oil*
- 1½ teaspoons salt

- 1 pound fresh Chinese egg noodles (about ⅓ inch in diameter) or fresh angel hair pasta
- 12 green onions (white and pale green parts only), thinly sliced
- ½ cup coarsely chopped roasted peanuts
- ¼ cup thinly sliced fresh Thai basil leaves or regular basil leaves

Heat peanut oil in small skillet over medium heat. Add ginger and garlic; sauté 1 minute. Transfer to large bowl. Add next 6 ingredients; whisk to blend.

Place noodles in sieve over sink. Separate noodles with fingers and shake to remove excess starch. Cook noodles in large pot of boiling salted water until just tender, stirring occasionally. Drain and rinse under cold water until cool. Drain thoroughly and transfer to bowl with sauce. Add sliced green onions and toss to coat noodles. Let stand at room temperature until noodles have absorbed dressing, tossing occasionally, about 1 hour. Stir in peanuts and Thai basil; toss again. Season to taste with salt and pepper. Serve noodles at room temperature.

**Sold in the Asian foods section of many supermarkets and at Asian markets.*

4 TO 6 SERVINGS

Pasta with Chicken, Curly Endive, and Blue Cheese

- 1 pound gnocchi-shaped pasta (such as cavatelli) or shell pasta
- 3 tablespoons olive oil
- 1 large red onion, halved, sliced crosswise
- 4 skinless boneless chicken breast halves, cut crosswise into 1/3- to 1/2-inch-thick slices
- 4 teaspoons chopped fresh rosemary
- 1 head of curly endive, trimmed, very coarsely chopped (about 12 cups)
- 1 1/2 cups crumbled blue cheese (such as Maytag; about 9 ounces)
- 3/4 cup coarsely chopped toasted walnuts (optional)

Cook pasta in large pot of boiling salted water until just tender but still firm to bite, stirring occasionally.

Meanwhile, heat oil in heavy large deep skillet over medium-high heat. Add onion; sauté until slightly softened, about 4 minutes. Sprinkle chicken with salt and pepper; add to skillet with rosemary and sauté until chicken is almost cooked through, about 4 minutes. Add endive; toss until slightly wilted and chicken is cooked through, about 1 minute.

Drain pasta, reserving 3/4 cup pasta cooking liquid. Return pasta to pot. Add chicken mixture, blue cheese, and enough pasta cooking liquid to moisten; toss to blend. Season with salt and pepper. Transfer to large bowl; sprinkle with nuts, if desired.

6 SERVINGS

Picnic at the Concert for 6

Spicy Sesame Noodles with Chopped Peanuts and Thai Basil
(opposite; pictured opposite)

Asian Coleslaw

Baby Carrots

Beer and *Lemonade*

Chocolate-Orange Cookie Stacks
(page 228)

Campanelle with Arugula, Tomatoes, and Feta

8 ounces campanelle (trumpet-shaped pasta) or fusilli (spiral-shaped pasta)

6 tablespoons extra-virgin olive oil, divided
6 green onions, chopped (about 1 cup)
3 large garlic cloves, minced
1 pint whole cherry tomatoes
1 pint whole grape tomatoes

5 cups (loosely packed) arugula
1½ cups crumbled feta cheese (about 7 ounces)

Cook pasta in large pot of boiling salted water until just tender but still firm to bite, stirring occasionally.

Meanwhile, heat 3 tablespoons olive oil in heavy large skillet over high heat. Add green onions, minced garlic, and all tomatoes; sauté until tomatoes begin to soften and collapse, about 7 minutes. Sprinkle tomato mixture with salt and pepper.

Drain pasta. Return to pot. Add tomato mixture, arugula, and remaining 3 tablespoons olive oil; toss until arugula begins to wilt. Season to taste with salt and pepper. Transfer pasta to plates. Sprinkle with feta cheese and serve.

4 SERVINGS

Fettuccine with Asparagus, Morels, and Tarragon

- 8 ounces fresh morel mushrooms, halved if large, or 1 ounce dried morels
- 3 tablespoons butter
- 1 cup (packed) sliced shallots
- 1 pound asparagus, trimmed, cut into 1½-inch lengths
- 1¼ cups vegetable broth (if using fresh morels)
- ⅔ cup whipping cream
- 2½ tablespoons chopped fresh tarragon, divided
- 12 ounces fettuccine
- 1 cup grated Parmesan cheese, divided

If using dried morels, place in 2-cup measuring cup and pour enough hot water over to reach 2-cup mark. Let soak until soft, pushing down occasionally if morels rise to top, about 20 minutes. Drain, reserving soaking liquid; add enough water to measure 1¼ cups if needed. Cut large morels in half.

Melt butter in heavy large skillet over medium-high heat. Add shallots and fresh or reconstituted morels; sauté until shallots are tender, about 6 minutes. Add asparagus and 1¼ cups broth (if using fresh morels) or reserved soaking liquid (if using dried morels). Bring to boil, cover, and cook 2 minutes. Stir in cream and 2 tablespoons chopped tarragon. Simmer uncovered until sauce thickens slightly, about 4 minutes. Season sauce to taste with salt and pepper.

Meanwhile, cook pasta in large pot of boiling salted water until just tender but still firm to bite, stirring occasionally. Drain pasta and return to pot. Add ½ cup Parmesan cheese and sauce; toss. Transfer to bowl; sprinkle with remaining ½ tablespoon tarragon. Serve with remaining Parmesan cheese.

4 SERVINGS

Dinner from the Trattoria for 4

Steamed Artichokes with Salsa Verde
(page 20)

Campanelle with Arugula, Tomatoes, and Feta
(opposite; pictured opposite)

Tricolore Salad

Soave

Biscotti

Chocolates

Vin Santo

Mac and Cheese with Buffalo Chicken

CHICKEN

- 2¼ cups all purpose flour
- 1½ tablespoons cayenne pepper
- 1½ tablespoons paprika
- 1½ tablespoons salt
- 1½ tablespoons ground cumin
- 1½ tablespoons ground coriander
- 2 cups whole milk
- 3 large eggs, beaten to blend
- 4 cups cornflakes, ground to crumbs in processor
- 1 pound chicken cutlets, cut crosswise into 1-inch-wide strips

Canola oil (for deep-frying)

MACARONI

- 1 pound small elbow macaroni
- 2 cups chopped green onions (about 8 large)
- 2 tablespoons chopped fresh oregano
- 8 tablespoons (1 stick) butter, divided
- 3 cups chopped onions
- 2 large garlic cloves, chopped
- ½ cup all purpose flour

4 cups whole milk
1 pound extra-sharp cheddar cheese, coarsely grated (about 4 cups packed)
8 ounces provolone cheese, coarsely grated (about 2 cups packed)
2 teaspoons paprika
1 teaspoon salt
1 teaspoon freshly ground black pepper

1 cup hot pepper sauce (preferably Frank's RedHot Original)

A comfort classic meets a bar-food favorite. Team it with carrots and celery sticks and a couple of six-packs of your favorite lager.

FOR CHICKEN: Whisk first 6 ingredients in deep medium bowl to blend. Place milk in second bowl, eggs in third bowl, and ground cornflakes in fourth bowl. Working with 4 chicken strips at a time, place in flour mixture and toss to coat. Dip same chicken strips into milk, then eggs, then cornflake crumbs, coating with each; arrange on sheet of foil.

Pour oil into heavy medium saucepan to depth of 2 inches. Attach deep-fry thermometer to side of pan; heat oil to 335°F to 350°F. Working in batches, add coated chicken strips to hot oil and fry until golden and cooked through, turning occasionally, about 3 minutes. Using slotted spoon, transfer chicken strips to paper towels to drain. Cut strips into 1-inch-long pieces.

FOR MACARONI: Cook macaroni in large pot of boiling salted water until just tender but still firm to bite. Drain; transfer to very large bowl. Mix in green onions and oregano. Melt 6 tablespoons butter in same large pot over medium heat. Add 3 cups chopped onions and garlic. Cover; sauté until onions are soft but not brown, stirring often, about 6 minutes. Add flour; stir 2 minutes. Gradually whisk in milk. Bring to boil, whisking constantly. Reduce heat and simmer sauce 2 minutes. Add all cheeses, paprika, 1 teaspoon salt, and 1 teaspoon pepper. Whisk until cheeses melt and sauce is smooth, about 2 minutes. Remove from heat. Season to taste with more salt and pepper, if desired. Mix cheese sauce into macaroni. Mix in chicken pieces. Mound mixture in 13x9x2-inch glass baking dish. *(Can be prepared 2 hours ahead. Let stand at room temperature.)*

Preheat oven to 350°F. Stir hot pepper sauce and remaining 2 tablespoons butter in small saucepan over medium heat until butter melts; spoon 4 tablespoons over macaroni in dish. Bake macaroni uncovered until heated through, about 30 minutes, or 45 minutes if made ahead. Serve, passing remaining butter and hot-sauce mixture separately.

12 SERVINGS

Sweet Pea and Artichoke Lasagna

- 2 8-ounce packages frozen artichoke hearts, thawed, coarsely chopped
- 1½ cups whipping cream, divided
- ¼ cup (packed) chopped fresh basil leaves
- 2 15-ounce containers whole-milk ricotta cheese
- 1 1-pound bag frozen petite peas, thawed
- ¾ cup grated Parmesan cheese
- 2 large eggs
- 1 teaspoon salt
- 1 8- to 9-ounce package no-boil lasagna noodles (12 noodles)
- 4 cups coarsely grated mozzarella cheese (about 1 pound)

Preheat oven to 400°F. Brush 13x9x2-inch glass baking dish with oil. Mix artichokes, ½ cup cream, and basil in medium bowl. Puree remaining 1 cup cream, ricotta, and next 4 ingredients in processor. Spread 1 cup ricotta mixture over bottom of prepared baking dish. Arrange 4 noodles in single layer over ricotta, breaking noodles as needed to cover. Spread half of artichoke mixture over. Spread 2½ cups ricotta mixture over artichokes. Sprinkle 1 cup mozzarella cheese over. Repeat with 4 noodles, artichoke mixture, 2½ cups ricotta mixture, and 1 cup mozzarella. Top with 4 noodles. Spread remaining ricotta mixture over, then sprinkle remaining 2 cups mozzarella cheese over. Tent with aluminium foil, sealing edges.

Bake lasagna 30 minutes. Remove foil; continue baking until bubbling at edges and brown on top, about 25 minutes. Let stand 15 minutes before serving.

10 TO 12 SERVINGS

Linguine with Shrimp, Asparagus, and Basil

- 8 ounces linguine

- 3 tablespoons olive oil
- 2 garlic cloves, chopped
- 1 tablespoon chopped red jalapeño chiles
- ½ cup dry white wine
- 1 tablespoon butter
- 12 uncooked large shrimp, peeled and deveined with tails intact
- 12 slender asparagus, trimmed, cut diagonally into 1½-inch pieces
- 1 tablespoon fresh lemon juice

- 2 cups (packed) fresh basil leaves, thinly sliced, plus additional for garnish
- 2 lemon wedges

Cook pasta in large pot of boiling salted water until just tender but still firm to bite, stirring occasionally.

Meanwhile, heat oil in heavy large skillet over medium-high heat. Add garlic and jalapeño; sauté 1 minute. Add wine and butter; boil 2 minutes. Add shrimp, asparagus, and lemon juice. Toss until asparagus is just tender and shrimp are just opaque, about 3 minutes.

Drain pasta and add to skillet; add 2 cups sliced basil leaves and toss until basil wilts and sauce coats pasta, about 1 minute. Season with salt and pepper. Divide pasta between 2 plates. Garnish with fresh basil leaves and lemon wedges and serve.

2 SERVINGS

Sunday Family Supper for 12

Antipasto Platter

Sweet Pea and Artichoke Lasagna
(opposite; pictured opposite)

Grilled Sausages

Mixed Green Salad

Breadsticks

Chianti

Pizzelle S'mores with Ice Cream and Chocolate Sauce
(page 218)

Three-Cheese Pizza with Pancetta and Mushrooms

- Pizza Dough (see recipe)
- ½ cup purchased marinara sauce
- 1 cup coarsely grated Fontina cheese
- ½ cup finely grated Parmesan cheese
- ⅓ cup coarsely grated mozzarella cheese
- 2 ounces crimini (baby bella) mushrooms, thinly sliced
- 2 ounces thinly sliced pancetta (Italian bacon), coarsely chopped

Preheat oven to 475°F. Line 2 large baking sheets with parchment. Divide dough in half. Roll out 1 half on lightly floured surface to 13½x8½-inch rectangle. Transfer to 1 baking sheet. Repeat with second half. Spread ¼ cup marinara sauce over each pizza, leaving ½-inch border. Sprinkle cheeses over, then mushrooms and pancetta. Sprinkle with salt and generous amount of pepper.

Bake pizzas until brown on bottom and cheese is melted, about 15 minutes. Cut each pizza crosswise into rectangles.

6 SERVINGS

Pizza Dough

- ¾ cup warm water (105°F to 115°F)
- 1 envelope active dry yeast
- 2 cups (or more) all purpose flour

1 teaspoon sugar
¾ teaspoon salt
3 tablespoons olive oil

This dough is easy to handle and will give you a crispy crust that's also tender.

Pour ¾ cup warm water into small bowl; stir in yeast. Let stand until yeast dissolves, about 5 minutes.

Brush large bowl lightly with olive oil. Mix 2 cups flour, sugar, and salt in processor. Add yeast mixture and 3 tablespoons oil; process until dough forms sticky ball. Transfer to lightly floured surface. Knead dough until smooth, adding more flour by tablespoonfuls if dough is very sticky, about 1 minute. Transfer to prepared bowl; turn dough in bowl to coat with oil. Cover bowl with plastic wrap; let dough rise in warm draft-free area until doubled in volume, about 1 hour. Punch down dough. *(Can be made 1 day ahead. Store in airtight container in refrigerator.)* Roll out dough, starting in center and working outward toward edges but not rolling over them.

Potato, Sage, and Rosemary Pizza

3 tablespoons extra-virgin olive oil
12 ounces unpeeled small Yukon Gold potatoes, sliced into very thin rounds
1 13.8-ounce tube refrigerated pizza dough
2 teaspoons chopped fresh rosemary
2 teaspoons chopped fresh sage
2 garlic cloves, chopped
¼ teaspoon dried crushed red pepper
1 cup (packed) grated whole-milk mozzarella cheese (about 4 ounces)
½ cup finely grated Parmesan cheese

Add a salad and your meal is set. Or serve small squares for an appetizer.

Preheat oven to 400°F. Heat oil in heavy large skillet over medium heat. Add potato slices in single layer. Sauté until just tender, about 5 minutes. Cool briefly.

Unroll dough on rimmed baking sheet. Scatter potato slices over dough, leaving ¾-inch plain border. Sprinkle with rosemary, sage, garlic, and crushed red pepper. Sprinkle with cheeses to cover.

Bake pizza until crust is crisp and cheeses melt, about 20 minutes. Using metal spatula, loosen crust from sheet. Slide out onto platter or board and serve.

4 SERVINGS

Grilled Pizza with Harissa and Herb Salad

DOUGH

1¼ cups warm water (105°F to 115°F)
¼ teaspoon sugar
1 envelope (¼ ounce) active dry yeast
3 cups (or more) all purpose flour, divided

¼ cup whole wheat flour
1 tablespoon extra-virgin olive oil plus additional for brushing
2½ teaspoons coarse kosher salt

6 teaspoons harissa sauce
1½ cups (packed) coarsely grated Gruyère cheese, divided
¾ cup freshly grated Parmesan cheese, divided

HERB SALAD

4 cups mixed baby greens
1 cup fresh Italian parsley leaves
1 cup fresh basil leaves, coarsely torn
½ cup coarsely chopped assorted fresh herbs (such as chives, chervil, tarragon, and dill)
1 tablespoon extra-virgin olive oil

¼ cup pine nuts, lightly toasted

FOR DOUGH: Mix 1¼ cups warm water and sugar in large bowl; sprinkle yeast over. Let stand until yeast dissolves and mixture looks spongey, about 10 minutes. Whisk in 1 cup all purpose flour; let stand in warm draft-free area until bubbling, about 35 minutes.

Stir whole wheat flour, 1 tablespoon olive oil, and coarse salt into yeast mixture, then stir in 2 cups all purpose flour. Knead dough in bowl until almost smooth and beginning to pull away from sides of bowl, adding more all purpose flour by tablespoonfuls if dough is very sticky. Turn dough out onto lightly floured surface and knead until smooth and elastic, about 7 minutes. Form dough into ball. Place dough ball in oiled large bowl; turn dough to coat with oil. Cover with plastic wrap and let dough rise in warm draft-free area until doubled in volume, about 1½ hours.

Punch down dough; divide into 6 equal pieces. Roll each dough piece on floured surface into ball. Cover dough balls loosely with plastic wrap and let rest 30 minutes.

Prepare barbecue (medium-high heat). Sprinkle 2 large baking sheets with flour. Roll out each dough ball on lightly floured work surface to 7- to 7½-inch round, letting dough rest briefly if springing back. Transfer to floured baking sheets. Brush tops lightly with olive oil. Working in batches, grill dough rounds, oiled side up, until bottoms are firm and grill marks appear, watching to avoid burning, about 3 minutes. Turn crusts over, grilling until dough is set, about 2 minutes. Transfer crusts, grill-marked side up, to baking sheets. *(Can be made 8 hours ahead. Let stand at room temperature.)*

Prepare barbecue (medium heat). Spread 1 teaspoon harissa very thinly over top of each pizza crust. Sprinkle each with 1/4 cup Gruyère and 2 tablespoons Parmesan cheese. Return pizzas to grill; cover and grill just until cheese melts, about 4 minutes.

FOR HERB SALAD: Combine baby greens, parsley leaves, basil leaves, chopped assorted fresh herbs, and olive oil in medium bowl; toss to coat thoroughly with oil.

Place pizzas on platter. Top with salad; sprinkle with pine nuts.

MAKES 6 INDIVIDUAL PIZZAS

***Harissa*, Tunisian hot sauce, is available at Middle Eastern markets and specialty foods stores. Purchased pizza dough can be used instead of homemade, if time is short.**

Pea Salad with Radishes and Feta Cheese (page 160)

On the Side

Side Dishes

Salads

Breads

Warm New Potatoes, Cherry Tomatoes, and Green Beans with Fresh Basil

Nonstick vegetable oil spray
2 pounds small new potatoes, halved
5 tablespoons (about) extra-virgin olive oil, divided
1 pound slender green beans, trimmed
1 12-ounce container cherry tomatoes, halved
3 garlic cloves, finely chopped
⅓ cup chopped fresh basil

Preheat oven to 400°F. Spray rimmed baking sheet with nonstick spray. Toss potatoes and 2 tablespoons oil in large bowl. Scatter on prepared sheet; sprinkle with salt and pepper. Roast until tender, stirring occasionally, about 50 minutes. Maintain oven temperature.

Meanwhile, cook green beans in large saucepan of boiling salted water until crisp-tender, about 3 minutes. Drain beans; pat dry.

Place beans, tomatoes, and garlic in large bowl. Add 2 tablespoons oil; sprinkle with salt and pepper and toss. Add to potatoes on sheet. Roast until tomatoes begin to break down, about 8 minutes. Sprinkle with basil; mix in 1 tablespoon oil, if desired. Mound warm vegetables in large shallow bowl.

8 SERVINGS

Molasses Baked Beans with Ginger

4 slices thick-cut bacon, cut crosswise into 1-inch pieces
1½ cups chopped onion
⅓ cup minced peeled fresh ginger
2 28-ounce cans original flavor baked beans
½ cup mild-flavored (light) molasses
2 tablespoons plus 2 teaspoons apple cider vinegar or distilled white vinegar

Set oven rack in lower middle position; preheat to 325°F. Heat heavy large pot over medium-high heat. Add bacon; cook until crisp, stirring often. Transfer to paper towels to drain. Pour off all but 2 tablespoons drippings from pot. Add onion; sauté until beginning to soften, about 5 minutes. Add ginger; sauté 1 minute. Stir in beans with juice, molasses, vinegar, and bacon; bring to simmer. Transfer to 11x7x2-inch glass baking dish. *(Can be made 1 day ahead. Cover and chill.)* Bake until top is dark brown and bubbling, about 2 hours. Let stand 15 minutes; serve.

8 SERVINGS

Grilled Corn on the Cob with Chile and Lime

- 6 tablespoons crema mexicana,* crème fraîche,* or sour cream
- 1 tablespoon fresh lime juice
- 1/4 teaspoon chipotle chile powder or ancho chile powder**
- 1/4 teaspoon coarse kosher salt

- 8 ears of corn with husks
- 2 limes, halved or quartered

- 1/4 cup chopped fresh cilantro

Mix crema mexicana, fresh lime juice, chile powder, and coarse kosher salt in small bowl to blend. *(Can be made 6 hours ahead. Cover and chill.)*

Prepare barbecue (medium heat). Remove outer husks from corn, leaving inner pale green husks attached. Fold back inner husks; remove corn silk. Sprinkle corn with salt and pepper. Rewrap inner husks around corn. Grill until husks are charred and beginning to pull away and corn is tender, turning often, about 10 minutes. Grill lime quarters until lightly charred, about 5 minutes.

Pull husks away from corn to expose kernels. Place corn and lime on platter. Brush corn with crema-lime mixture. Sprinkle with cilantro.

*Crema mexicana *(Mexican crème fraîche) is available at some supermarkets and in the refrigerated section of Latin markets. Crème fraîche is sold at some supermarkets and at specialty foods stores.*

***Chipotle and ancho chile powders are available in the spice section of many supermarkets.*

8 SERVINGS

Stubborn strands of corn silk are most easily removed by rubbing with a damp paper towel, or even with a little oil.

Sautéed Baby Beets with Haricots Verts and Lemon

- 10 red or golden baby beets, trimmed, scrubbed
- 2 tablespoons olive oil
- 1½ pounds haricots verts (slender green beans), trimmed
- ¼ cup (½ stick) butter
- 2 tablespoons fresh lemon juice
- 1½ teaspoons finely grated lemon peel
- ½ cup fresh Italian parsley leaves

Baby beets, which are roughly the size of a large marble, are sweeter than mature beets and cook more quickly.

Preheat oven to 375°F. Toss beets with oil in roasting pan. Sprinkle with salt. Cover pan with foil. Bake until beets are tender, about 30 minutes. Uncover and let beets stand at room temperature 20 minutes. Peel beets. Cut beets into quarters (or halves if very small).

Cook haricots verts in large pot of boiling salted water until crisp-tender, about 4 minutes. Drain and transfer to bowl of ice water to cool. Drain and pat dry. Melt butter in large skillet over medium heat. Add lemon juice and peel, then beets. Toss well. Stir in haricots verts and parsley; sauté until heated through, about 3 minutes. Season to taste with salt and pepper. Serve hot or at room temperature.

6 SERVINGS

Baby Bok Choy with Braised Shiitake Sauce

10 large dried shiitake mushrooms* (about 1½ ounces)
3 tablespoons vegetable oil, divided
8 baby bok choy,* halved lengthwise

1 teaspoon tapioca starch* or cornstarch
1 tablespoon water
1 large garlic clove, minced
1 cup low-salt chicken broth
1 tablespoon soy sauce
1 tablespoon oyster sauce*
1 tablespoon Asian sesame oil
1 teaspoon sugar
1 1-inch piece fresh ginger, peeled, cut into very thin matchstick-size strips (about 2 tablespoons)

Pour enough hot water over shiitakes to cover; let soak until soft, 45 minutes. Drain; squeeze to remove excess water. Cut off stems; discard. Thinly slice caps. Bring large pot of salted water to boil. Add 2 tablespoons oil, then bok choy; cook just until wilted, 30 seconds. Drain. Transfer to platter; cover.

Whisk 1 teaspoon tapioca starch and 1 tablespoon water in bowl. Heat 1 tablespoon oil in small skillet over medium-high heat. Add garlic; stir 30 seconds. Add shiitakes; stir 1 minute. Reduce heat to medium; add broth and next 4 ingredients. Whisk in tapioca mixture; cook until sauce thickens, about 30 seconds. Season with salt and pepper. Pour over bok choy; scatter ginger over.

**Avaiable at Asian markets and in the Asian section of some supermarkets.*

8 SERVINGS

Green Beans with Sweet and Sour Red Onions

1 pound slender green beans, trimmed
3 tablespoons butter
1 very large (14- to 16-ounce) red onion, peeled, halved lengthwise, sliced lengthwise
1 tablespoon chopped fresh marjoram
½ teaspoon dried crushed red pepper
⅓ cup red wine vinegar
2 tablespoons (packed) dark brown sugar

Steam beans until crisp-tender, about 5 minutes. Transfer to plate. Melt butter in heavy large skillet over high heat. Add next 3 ingredients. Sauté until onion begins to soften, about 2 minutes. Add vinegar and sugar. Stir until sauce thickens, about 1½ minutes. Add beans; toss to coat and heat through, about 1 minute. Season with salt and pepper. Mound in shallow bowl.

6 SERVINGS

Salt and Pepper Oven Fries

- 3 large baking potatoes (about 2 pounds) peeled, cut lengthwise into ½-inch-wide planks, each plank cut lengthwise into ½-inch-wide strips
- 2 tablespoons olive oil
- 1 teaspoon sea salt
- 1 teaspoon shichimi togarashi*
- 1 teaspoon sugar

Place rack in top third of oven and preheat to 400°F. Place potato strips on rimmed baking sheet. Drizzle with olive oil; toss to coat. Roast 25 minutes. Using spatula, turn fries over. Roast until tender and golden brown around edges, about 25 minutes longer. Mix salt, shichimi, and sugar in small bowl. Sprinkle over fries.

**A Japanese table seasoning that includes dried chiles, sesame seeds, and seaweed; available in the Asian foods section of some supermarkets and at Japanese markets.*

6 SERVINGS

Steak and Potatoes Dinner for 6

Shrimp Cocktail

Martinis

Porcini-Crusted Filet Mignon with Tarragon-Chive Butter
(page 51)

Salt and Pepper Oven Fries
(at left; pictured at left)

Creamed Spinach

Cabernet Sauvignon

Chocolate Bread Pudding with Walnuts and Chocolate Chips
(page 214)

Cognac

Potato-Onion Gratin

- 3 tablespoons olive oil, divided, plus more for brushing
- 4 cups thinly sliced onions
- 3 large garlic cloves, chopped
- 1 tablespoon chopped fresh thyme
- 1 teaspoon chopped fresh rosemary
- 2 pounds Yukon Gold potatoes, peeled, sliced into 1/8-inch-thick rounds
- 3/4 teaspoon salt
- 3/4 teaspoon coarsely ground black pepper
- 1 1/4 cups low-salt chicken broth

Heat 2 tablespoons oil in large skillet over medium-high heat. Add onions and garlic; sprinkle with salt and pepper. Sauté until onions are golden, about 8 minutes. Add herbs; sauté 2 minutes. *(Can be made 2 hours ahead. Let stand at room temperature.)*

Preheat oven to 425°F. Brush 11x7x2-inch glass baking dish with oil. Arrange 1/3 of potatoes in dish. Sprinkle with 1/4 teaspoon each salt and pepper. Top potatoes with half of onion mixture. Repeat; top with potatoes. Pour broth over. Drizzle with 1 tablespoon oil.

Cover dish with foil. Bake potatoes 30 minutes. Uncover and continue to bake until potatoes are tender and top is golden, about 25 minutes longer. Let stand 10 minutes and serve.

(Taken from *Gordon Ramsay's Sunday Lunch*, published by Quadrille Publishing).

6 SERVINGS

Grilled Garlic-Marinated Baby Zucchini

- 1/2 cup olive oil
- 4 garlic cloves, peeled
- 1/2 teaspoon coarse kosher salt plus additional for sprinkling
- 1/4 teaspoon ground black pepper
- 1 pound baby zucchini, trimmed

Blend first 4 ingredients in blender until almost smooth. Using fork or wooden skewer, pierce zucchini all over. Place in medium bowl. Pour garlic oil over zucchini and let stand at room temperature at least 30 minutes and up to 1 hour, tossing occasionally.

Prepare barbecue (medium-high heat). Grill zucchini until tender and golden in spots, turning occasionally, about 6 minutes. Transfer to plate, sprinkle with additional salt, and serve.

6 SERVINGS

Jasmine Rice with Garlic, Ginger, and Cilantro

- 3 cups jasmine rice*
- 3 tablespoons vegetable oil
- 1/3 cup finely chopped peeled fresh ginger
- 3 large garlic cloves, minced
- 4 1/2 cups low-salt chicken broth
- 3/4 teaspoon salt
- 1 large bunch fresh cilantro, coarsely chopped

Place rice in large sieve; rinse under cold running water until water runs clear. Drain. Heat oil in heavy large saucepan over medium-high heat. Add ginger and garlic; stir until fragrant, about 30 seconds. Add rice and stir 3 minutes. Stir in broth and salt. Sprinkle cilantro over. Bring to boil. Reduce heat to medium-low; cover and cook until rice is tender, about 18 minutes. Remove from heat; let stand covered 10 minutes. Fluff rice with fork. Transfer to bowl and serve.

**Available at Asian markets and in the Asian section of some supermarkets.*

8 SERVINGS

Sautéed Zucchini, Cherry Tomatoes, Olives, and Basil

- 2 tablespoons extra-virgin olive oil
- 1 1/4 to 1 1/2 pounds zucchini, trimmed, cut into 1/2-inch-thick slices
- 2 large garlic cloves, sliced
- 1 1/2 teaspoons chopped fresh rosemary
- 2 cups small cherry tomatoes, halved
- 1/3 cup halved pitted Kalamata olives
- 1/4 cup thinly sliced fresh basil
- 1 tablespoon balsamic vinegar

Heat oil in large skillet over medium-high heat. Add zucchini, garlic, and rosemary. Sprinkle with salt and pepper. Sauté until zucchini is just tender, about 5 minutes. Add tomatoes and olives. Sauté until tomatoes just begin to soften, about 2 minutes. Mix in basil and vinegar. Season vegetables to taste with salt and pepper. Transfer to bowl.

(Taken from *Gordon Ramsay's Sunday Lunch*, published by Quadrille Publishing).

6 SERVINGS

Roasted Cauliflower with Onions and Fennel

- 1 medium head of Romanesco or regular cauliflower (about 1¼ pounds), cored, cut into 1-inch florets
- 6 tablespoons olive oil, divided
- 2 medium onions (about ½ pound each), halved lengthwise, cut into ¾-inch-wide wedges with some core still attached, peeled
- 2 fresh fennel bulbs (about 1 pound total), halved lengthwise, cut lengthwise into ½-inch-wide wedges with some core still attached
- 8 small garlic cloves, unpeeled
- 15 fresh marjoram sprigs

Position rack in center of oven; preheat to 425°F. Toss cauliflower and 2 tablespoons oil in large bowl. Heat heavy large skillet over medium-high heat. Add cauliflower and sauté until beginning to brown, about 5 minutes. Transfer cauliflower to rimmed baking sheet.

Add 2 tablespoons oil to same skillet. Add onion wedges. Cook until browned on 1 side, about 3 minutes. Using spatula, carefully transfer onions to baking sheet with cauliflower, arranging wedges browned side up. Add 2 tablespoons oil to same skillet. Add fennel; sauté until fennel softens slightly and starts to brown, about 5 minutes. Transfer to same baking sheet. Scatter garlic and marjoram over vegetables. Sprinkle with salt and pepper. Roast until caramelized, about 25 minutes. Serve hot or at room temperature.

6 SERVINGS

Fresh Spinach with Garlic-Yogurt Sauce

- 4 tablespoons olive oil, divided
- 2/3 cup chopped onion
- 1/2 tablespoon tomato paste
- 4 dried chiles de árbol*
- 1 1/2 pounds fresh spinach leaves (four 6-ounce bags), divided
- 1 1/2 tablespoons uncooked medium-grain white rice

- 2 garlic cloves
- 6 tablespoons plain Greek yogurt or drained plain whole-milk yogurt
- 1 tablespoon butter
- 1/2 teaspoon cayenne pepper

Heat 3 tablespoons oil in heavy large skillet over medium heat. Add onion and sauté until translucent, about 5 minutes. Add tomato paste; stir 1 minute. Add chiles and 1/3 of spinach. Cook until spinach wilts, adding remaining spinach in 2 additions and tossing often, about 4 minutes. Mix in rice. Cover and simmer until rice is tender and moisture from spinach is absorbed, adding water by tablespoonfuls if needed for rice, about 10 minutes. Uncover and continue to cook until mixture is dry, about 2 minutes; discard chiles.

Meanwhile, press garlic cloves into small bowl, stir in yogurt, and season with salt and pepper. Melt butter with 1 tablespoon oil in small skillet. Mix in cayenne pepper and remove from heat.

Spread spinach on platter; make indentations with back of spoon. Spoon yogurt into indentations and drizzle with cayenne butter.

**Small, thin, very hot red chiles; available at some supermarkets and at Latin markets.*

6 SERVINGS

Cauliflower, White Bean, and Feta Salad

- 1/3 cup olive oil
- 1 teaspoon minced fresh rosemary
- 2 tablespoons fresh lemon juice
- 1 tablespoon red wine vinegar
- 2 1/2 teaspoons finely grated lemon peel
- 1 1/2 teaspoons salt
- 1/2 teaspoon ground black pepper

- 1 medium head of cauliflower, trimmed, cut into small florets (about 3 cups)
- 1 15-ounce can white beans (such as Great Northern or navy beans), drained
- 2 large heads of Belgian endive, trimmed, halved lengthwise, then thinly sliced crosswise
- 1 tablespoon chopped fresh chives
- 2 teaspoons chopped fresh parsley
- 1/2 cup crumbled feta cheese (about 3 ounces)

Combine oil and rosemary in small saucepan. Stir over medium heat just until fragrant, about 1 minute. Cool. Whisk lemon juice and next 4 ingredients in small bowl.

Combine cauliflower, beans, endive, chives, parsley, and rosemary oil in medium bowl; toss. Mix in cheese. Add lemon juice mixture and toss. Season salad with salt and pepper.

6 SERVINGS

Grapefruit and Avocado Salad with Ginger-Cassis Dressing

3 tablespoons extra-virgin olive oil
3 tablespoons crème de cassis (black-currant liqueur) or grenadine
2 tablespoons chopped shallots
2 tablespoons minced peeled fresh ginger
4 teaspoons Sherry wine vinegar

2 large Ruby Red grapefruits
1 large head of butter lettuce, leaves separated
1 large avocado, halved, pitted, peeled, sliced

Whisk first 5 ingredients in small bowl to blend. Season dressing very generously with salt and pepper.

Cut off peel and white pith from grapefruits. Cut each grapefruit crosswise into 4 slices, then cut each slice crosswise in half. Arrange lettuce leaves on platter, tearing large ones in half. Top with grapefruit and avocado. Drizzle with dressing; sprinkle with salt and pepper.

6 SERVINGS

Dinner Under the Stars for 6

Gazpacho

Grilled Halibut with Basil-Shallot Butter
(page 94)

Cauliflower, White Bean, and Feta Salad
(opposite; pictured opposite)

French Bread

Chablis

Plum Tarte Tatin
(page 185)

Arugula and Peach Salad with Creamy Chive Vinaigrette

- 2 large ripe peaches
- 2 tablespoons fresh lemon juice, divided
- 6 tablespoons extra-virgin olive oil
- 1½ tablespoons whipping cream
- ⅓ cup finely chopped fresh chives

- 12 cups (loosely packed) arugula (about 6 ounces)

Wash peaches, rubbing to remove fuzz. Cut in half; remove pits. Thinly slice peaches. Place in large bowl. Add ½ tablespoon lemon juice; toss. Whisk 1½ tablespoons lemon juice and olive oil in small bowl. Whisk in cream, then chives. Season with salt and pepper.

Add arugula to bowl with peaches. Add dressing and toss. Season with more salt and pepper, if desired, and serve.

6 SERVINGS

Mâche and Avocado Salad with Tortilla Strips

- 1/4 cup plus 3 tablespoons extra-virgin olive oil
- 5 6-inch-diameter corn tortillas, each cut into 3x1/2-inch strips
- 2 tablespoons fresh lime juice
- 1 tablespoon chopped shallot
- 1 1/2 teaspoons honey

- 10 cups (loosely packed) mâche or baby spinach
- 1 avocado, peeled, pitted, cut lengthwise into 1/4-inch-thick strips

Heat 1/4 cup oil in heavy large skillet over medium-high heat. Working in batches, fry tortilla strips until golden, about 2 minutes. Transfer to paper towels. Sprinkle with salt. Whisk lime juice, shallot, and honey in small bowl. Whisk in 3 tablespoons oil. Season with salt and pepper. *(Can be made 1 day ahead. Cool strips completely and store in airtight container at room temperature. Cover and chill dressing.)*

Place mâche and avocado in large bowl. Add dressing; toss. Season with salt and pepper. Top with tortilla strips.

6 SERVINGS

Arugula Salad with Olives, Pancetta, and Parmesan Shavings

- 6 thin slices pancetta (Italian bacon; about 1⁄3 of 3-ounce package)

- 1 1⁄2 tablespoons extra-virgin olive oil
- 1 tablespoon fresh lemon juice
- 4 cups (loosely packed) arugula
- 1⁄3 cup Kalamata olives, pitted, halved
- Parmesan cheese shavings

Arrange pancetta in single layer in medium nonstick skillet. Cook over medium heat until browned and crisp (do not turn), about 8 minutes. Transfer to paper towels to drain.

Whisk oil and lemon juice in small bowl. Season dressing with salt and pepper. Place arugula and olives in medium bowl; toss with dressing. Divide salad between plates. Top with pancetta and Parmesan shavings.

2 SERVINGS

Cabbage and Corn Slaw with Cilantro and Orange Dressing

- 1/3 cup frozen orange juice concentrate, thawed
- 1/3 cup unseasoned rice vinegar
- 1/3 cup canola oil or vegetable oil

- 2 8-ounce bags coleslaw mix
- 4 ears of fresh corn, shucked, kernels cut from cob
- 2 medium carrots, peeled, coarsely grated
- 1 medium red bell pepper, stemmed, cored, cut into thin strips
- 6 medium green onions, thinly sliced
- 1/2 cup chopped fresh cilantro

Whisk orange juice concentrate, rice vinegar, and canola oil in small bowl. Season with salt and pepper. *(Dressing can be made 1 day ahead. Cover and refrigerate.)*

Combine slaw mix, corn kernels, carrots, red bell pepper strips, sliced green onions, and chopped cilantro in large bowl. Toss with enough dressing to coat. Season slaw to taste with salt and pepper. Let stand 15 minutes for flavors to blend. Toss again and serve.

8 SERVINGS

Escarole Salad with White Beans and Lime Vinaigrette

- 3 tablespoons olive oil
- 2 tablespoons fresh lime juice
- 1 serrano chile, minced
- 8 cups escarole salad mix (about 7 ounces)
- 1 15-ounce can cannellini (white kidney beans), drained, rinsed
- 1/2 cup Kalamata olives, pitted, halved
- 1/4 cup toasted pepitas (pumpkin seeds) or pine nuts

Whisk first 3 ingredients in small bowl. Season dressing with salt and pepper. Toss salad mix, cannellini, and olives in large bowl. Pour dressing over; toss. Divide salad among plates. Sprinkle with pepitas or pine nuts and serve.

6 SERVINGS

Fireside Dinner for 4

Goat Cheese with Thyme, Peppercorns, and Lemon Oil
(page 15)

Rosemary-Roasted Rack of Lamb and Cherry Tomatoes
(page 60)

Arugula Salad with Olives Pancetta, and Parmesan Shavings
(double recipe; opposite; pictured opposite)

Roasted Potatoes

Merlot

Quick Chocolate-Cinnamon Mousse with Cherries
(page 216)

Artichoke, Fennel, and Crispy Prosciutto Salad

4 tablespoons olive oil, divided
2 tablespoons red wine vinegar
1 small shallot, finely chopped
1 tablespoon chopped fresh parsley
1 teaspoon Dijon mustard
1 teaspoon chopped fresh thyme

6 ounces thinly sliced prosciutto, cut crosswise into ⅓-inch-wide strips (about 1½ cups)

1 lemon, halved, plus 2 tablespoons fresh lemon juice
4 large artichokes

1 large fennel bulb with fronds, bulb halved lengthwise and very thinly sliced crosswise, fronds chopped
2 medium heads of frisée, torn into bite-size pieces

Whisk 3 tablespoons olive oil and next 5 ingredients in small bowl. Season dressing to taste with salt and pepper.

Heat remaining 1 tablespoon oil in nonstick medium skillet over medium-high heat. Add prosciutto and sauté until crisp, about 4 minutes. Transfer prosciutto to paper towels.

Fill medium bowl with cold water. Squeeze juice from lemon halves into water; add lemon halves. Cut off stem from 1 artichoke, then bend back all outer leaves and snap off where leaves break naturally (only small cone of pale green inner leaves will remain). Trim off all dark green parts. Cut out and discard choke. Slice artichoke bottom very thinly. Place in lemon water. Repeat with remaining 3 artichokes. *(Dressing, prosciutto, and artichokes can be made 2 hours ahead. Let stand at room temperature.)*

Drain artichokes well; transfer to large bowl. Add 2 tablespoons lemon juice and sliced fennel; toss. Mix in frisée and dressing; toss. Season salad with salt and pepper. Sprinkle with prosciutto and chopped fennel fronds and serve.

6 SERVINGS

Creamy Potato Salad with Lemon and Fresh Herbs

Because they are lower in starch than Yukon Golds or russets, baby red potatoes hold their shape when tossed.

3 pounds baby red potatoes

3 tablespoons unseasoned rice vinegar
3/4 cup mayonnaise
3 medium green onions, thinly sliced
1 celery stalk, cut into 1/3-inch cubes
1/4 cup chopped fresh parsley
1/4 cup chopped fresh basil
2 tablespoons chopped fresh dill
1 1/2 teaspoons finely grated lemon peel

Bring potatoes to boil in large pot of water. Reduce heat to medium-low and simmer until potatoes are tender, about 17 minutes. Drain; let stand until cool enough to handle, about 20 minutes.

Cut potatoes into 3/4-inch pieces. Place 1 layer of potatoes in large bowl; sprinkle with some of vinegar and salt and pepper. Continue layering potatoes with vinegar, salt, and pepper. Add all remaining ingredients; toss. Season with salt and pepper. *(Can be made 8 hours ahead. Cover and chill.)*

8 SERVINGS

Green Bean, Orange, and Green Olive Salad

2 tablespoons olive oil
1 tablespoon red wine vinegar
1 teaspoon honey
12 ounces haricots verts or small slender green beans, trimmed

2 oranges, all peel and white pith cut away
1/2 cup small green olives (such as picholine)
1/2 cup fresh Italian parsley leaves

Whisk first 3 ingredients in small bowl. Season with salt and pepper. Cook beans in large saucepan of boiling salted water until crisp-tender, about 3 minutes. Drain, rinse, and pat dry. *(Dressing and beans can be prepared 2 hours ahead. Let stand at room temperature.)*

Cut oranges in half, then crosswise into 1/3-inch-thick slices; place in large bowl. Mix in olives, parsley, beans, and dressing. Transfer to shallow dish.

6 SERVINGS

Grilled Zucchini and Bell Pepper Fattoush

- 3 medium orange or red bell peppers (about 1 pound), stemmed, seeded, quartered
- 4 to 5 slender zucchini (about 1 pound), trimmed, cut lengthwise in half
- 2 5- to 6-inch pita breads, each cut horizontally into 2 disks, or two 6x4x½-inch slices country white bread
- Olive oil (for grilling)

- 1 8-ounce cucumber, peeled, halved, seeded, cut into ½-inch cubes
- 12 cherry tomatoes, each halved
- 3 green onions, thinly sliced
- 1 cup (scant) pitted Kalamata olives, halved
- ½ cup (packed) fresh mint leaves
- ⅓ cup chopped fresh cilantro
- ½ cup olive oil
- ¼ cup fresh lemon juice
- 1 teaspoon ground cumin
- 1 4-ounce piece feta cheese, cut into ½-inch cubes (scant 1 cup)

- Ground sumac* (optional)

Prepare barbecue (medium heat). Brush peppers, zucchini, and bread on both sides with oil. Sprinkle lightly with salt and pepper. Grill peppers and zucchini until slightly charred and just tender, turning often, about 6 minutes. Transfer vegetables to foil-lined baking sheet. Grill bread until lightly charred and just crisp, turning often, about 3 minutes. Transfer to sheet with vegetables and cool. Tear bread into 1-inch pieces. *(Vegetables and bread can be made 2 hours ahead. Let stand at room temperature.)*

Cut peppers lengthwise into 1/2-inch-wide strips, then crosswise into 1/2-inch pieces. Cut zucchini lengthwise in half, then crosswise into 1/2-inch pieces. Place in large bowl. Add cucumber, tomatoes, green onions, olives, mint, and cilantro and toss to combine. Add bread pieces. Whisk 1/2 cup oil, lemon juice, and cumin in small bowl to blend. Season dressing to taste with salt and pepper. Add dressing to salad; toss to coat. Add feta and gently mix into salad.

Transfer salad to large bowl. Serve, passing ground sumac for sprinkling over, if desired.

**A fruity, tangy seasoning powder made from ground dried sumac berries; available at Middle Eastern markets.*

4 TO 6 SERVINGS

Fattoush **is a Middle Eastern take on *panzanella*, Italian bread salad. In fact, rustic Italian bread is a good alternative to the pita.**

Bibb Lettuce and Fresh Herb Salad with Roquefort

- 6 tablespoons red wine vinegar
- 3 tablespoons Dijon mustard
- 1 cup plus 2 tablespoons canola oil
- 1/3 cup (packed) fresh tarragon leaves
- 1/3 cup (packed) fresh chervil leaves
- 1/3 cup (packed) chopped Italian parsley
- 3 tablespoons chopped fresh chives
- 3 tablespoons minced shallots
- 1 tablespoon fresh lemon juice

- 3 heads of Bibb lettuce, cored, leaves coarsely torn
- 1 1/4 cups (about 5 ounces) coarsely crumbled Roquefort cheese, divided
- 1/2 cup pine nuts, toasted, divided

Whisk vinegar and mustard in small bowl. Gradually whisk in oil, herbs, shallots, and lemon juice. Season dressing to taste with salt and pepper. *(Can be made 2 hours ahead; let stand at room temperature.)*

Place lettuce, half of cheese, and half of nuts in very large bowl. Toss with enough dressing to coat. Sprinkle with remaining cheese and nuts.

12 SERVINGS

Hoppin' John Salad with Molasses Dressing

- 1/4 cup apple cider vinegar
- 1/4 cup mild-flavored (light) molasses
- 1/4 cup olive oil
- 1/4 teaspoon cayenne pepper
- 1 1-pound bag frozen black-eyed peas
- 1 1/2 cups 1/2-inch cubes peeled yam (red-skinned sweet potato)
- 2 cups 1/2-inch cubes andouille sausage (about 12 ounces)
- 1 1/2 cups frozen sliced okra, thawed, patted dry
- 1 cup chopped red onion

Whisk first 4 ingredients in small bowl to blend; season with salt and pepper. Cook black-eyed peas and yam in large saucepan of boiling salted water until tender, about 8 minutes. Drain; cool. Place in large bowl. Add andouille sausage, okra, and onion. Add enough dressing to coat and toss.

6 TO 8 SERVINGS

Pea Salad with Radishes and Feta Cheese

- 2 teaspoons cumin seeds
- 2 tablespoons fresh lime juice
- 2 teaspoons honey
- 1/4 cup extra-virgin olive oil
- 3 tablespoons chopped fresh dill

- 4 cups fresh shelled peas (from about 4 pounds peas in pods) or 1 pound frozen petite peas
- 1 bunch radishes, trimmed, halved, thinly sliced
- 1 cup crumbled feta cheese (about 4 ounces)
- 3 cups fresh pea tendrils, coarsely chopped, or pea sprouts* (optional)

Heat small skillet over medium heat. Add cumin seeds and toast until aromatic and slightly darker, about 2 minutes. Cool; grind finely in spice mill. Whisk lime juice, honey, and cumin in small bowl. Gradually whisk in oil; stir in dill. Season with salt and pepper. *(Can be made 1 day ahead. Cover and chill. Bring to room temperature.)*

Cook peas in pot of boiling salted water until almost tender, about 5 minutes for fresh (or about 2 minutes for frozen). Drain; rinse under cold water, then drain well. Transfer to large bowl. Add radishes, feta, and dressing; toss. Season with salt and pepper. Divide salad among bowls. If using pea tendrils or sprouts, divide among bowls and serve.

**Available at natural foods stores and Asian markets.*

4 TO 6 SERVINGS

Frisée and Fresh Herb Salad with Kumquats and Shiitake Mushrooms

- 1/4 cup white balsamic vinegar
- 1 large shallot, minced
- 1/2 cup plus 2 tablespoons extra-virgin olive oil
- 6 ounces small fresh shiitake mushrooms, stemmed
- 8 cups (lightly packed) torn frisée
- 1 cup fresh Italian parsley leaves
- 1/2 cup coarsely chopped fresh chives
- 6 kumquats, sliced into rounds, seeded (optional)

Combine vinegar and shallot in large bowl. Gradually whisk in 1/2 cup oil. Season dressing with salt and pepper. *(Can be made 6 hours ahead. Cover; chill. Bring to room temperature before using.)*

Heat 2 tablespoons oil in large skillet over medium-high heat. Add mushrooms; sprinkle with salt and pepper and sauté 5 minutes; cool. Add frisée, parsley, chives, and kumquats (if using) to dressing; toss. Mix in mushrooms. Season with more salt and pepper, if desired, and serve.

8 SERVINGS

Backyard Barbecue for 6

Deviled Eggs with Horseradish and Black Pepper
(halve recipe; page 16)

Barbecued Pork Sandwiches with Pickled Red Onion
(page 64)

Hoppin' John Salad with Molasses Dressing
(opposite; pictured opposite)

Coleslaw

Beer and *Lemonade*

Summer Peach Pie with Vanilla and Cardamom
(page 172)

Cranberry-Cornmeal Quick Bread

Nonstick vegetable oil spray
1 cup unbleached all purpose flour
1 cup white whole wheat flour or regular whole wheat flour
1 cup medium-grind whole grain cornmeal or regular cornmeal
½ cup sugar
1½ teaspoons salt
1½ teaspoons baking powder
1¼ cups buttermilk
½ cup (1 stick) unsalted butter, melted
½ cup pure maple syrup
2 large eggs
½ teaspoon maple extract
¾ cup chopped pecans plus 10 pecan halves for garnish
¾ cup dried cranberries (about 4 ounces)

Position rack in center of oven and preheat to 350°F. Spray 9x5x3-inch metal loaf pan with nonstick spray. Whisk both flours, cornmeal, sugar, salt, and baking powder in large bowl. Whisk buttermilk, melted butter, maple syrup, eggs, and maple extract in medium bowl. Add buttermilk mixture to flour mixture; stir just until blended. Stir in 3/4 cup chopped pecans and cranberries. Spoon batter into pan. Arrange pecan halves in row down center of batter.

Bake bread until top is golden brown and paring knife inserted into center of bread comes out clean, tenting bread loosely with foil if browning too quickly, about 1 hour 10 minutes. Cool in pan on rack 20 minutes. Turn out onto rack; cool. *(Can be made 1 day ahead. Wrap bread in foil and store at room temperature.)*

MAKES 1 LOAF

Blueberry Bran Muffins

Nonstick vegetable oil spray
2 cups unbleached all purpose flour
1 tablespoon coarse kosher salt
1 teaspoon baking powder
1 teaspoon baking soda
2 cups sour cream
1 cup sugar
1 cup vegetable oil
1 cup robust-flavored (dark) molasses
3 large eggs
6 cups wheat bran*
2 cups frozen blueberries (do not thaw)

Preheat oven to 350°F. Spray twelve 1-cup muffin cups with nonstick spray. Whisk flour, salt, baking powder, and baking soda in medium bowl. Whisk sour cream, sugar, oil, molasses, and eggs in large bowl. Whisk in dry ingredients. Add wheat bran and stir until almost blended. Add frozen berries and stir until evenly distributed. Divide batter equally among prepared muffin cups, about 2/3 cup each.

Bake muffins until tester inserted into center comes out with a few moist crumbs attached, about 37 minutes. Cool 10 minutes. Transfer muffins to rack and cool completely. *(Can be made 8 hours ahead. Let stand at room temperature.)*

**Available at natural foods stores.*

12 LARGE MUFFINS

Sunday Brunch for 12

Scrambled Eggs

Bacon

Sliced Melon

Cranberry-Cornmeal Quick Bread
(opposite; pictured opposite)

Blueberry Bran Muffins
(at left)

Apple Spice Cake with Brown Sugar Glaze
(page 200)

Orange Juice, Coffee, and *Tea*

Dipping Biscuits

- 2½ cups white whole wheat flour or regular whole wheat flour
- ½ cup unbleached bread flour
- 2½ teaspoons baking powder
- ¾ teaspoon salt
- ¾ teaspoon onion powder
- ½ teaspoon baking soda
- ½ teaspoon dried ground thyme
- ½ teaspoon dried rubbed sage
- ¾ cup (1½ sticks) chilled unsalted butter, cut into ½-inch cubes
- 1 cup buttermilk plus additional for brushing biscuit tops
- 1 large egg

Position rack in center of oven and preheat to 400°F. Line large rimmed baking sheet with parchment paper. Whisk whole wheat flour, bread flour, baking powder, salt, onion powder, baking soda, thyme, and sage in large bowl to blend. Add butter and rub in with fingertips until mixture resembles coarse meal. Whisk 1 cup buttermilk and egg in small bowl to blend. Add to flour mixture and mix with fork until evenly moistened (dough will be slightly sticky).

Turn biscuit dough out onto floured work surface. Knead briefly just until dough comes together, about 4 turns. Gather dough into ball. Using hands, flatten dough to ¾-inch-thick round. Using 2-inch-diameter biscuit cutter or cookie cutter dipped in flour, cut out

rounds. Transfer to prepared baking sheet, spacing 1 to 1½ inches apart. Gather dough scraps; flatten to ¾-inch thickness and cut out additional rounds. Brush tops of biscuits with additional buttermilk.

Bake biscuits until tops are light golden and tester inserted into centers comes out clean, about 22 minutes. Transfer biscuits to rack. Serve warm or at room temperature. *(Can be made 8 hours ahead. Cool biscuits completely, then wrap in foil and store at room temperature. Rewarm foil-wrapped biscuits in 350°F oven about 10 minutes, if desired, or serve at room temperature.)*

MAKES ABOUT 16

Flavored with traditional stuffing herbs, these are great for mopping up gravy. They also make a tasty snack sandwich with leftover turkey and chicken.

Grilled Flatbreads with Za'atar

- 1¼ cups warm water (105°F to 115°F)
- 1 teaspoon active dry yeast
- 3 cups (or more) all purpose flour
- 2 teaspoons coarse kosher salt
- 5 tablespoons (about) olive oil, divided
- 2 tablespoons za'atar*

Place 1¼ cups warm water in small bowl. Sprinkle yeast over. Let stand until yeast dissolves, about 10 minutes. Whisk 3 cups flour and salt in large bowl. Add yeast mixture and 2 tablespoons oil. Using wooden spoon, mix until sticky dough forms. Turn out onto floured surface. Knead until smooth and elastic, sprinkling with more flour if very sticky, about 6 minutes.

Oil another large bowl. Add dough; turn to coat. Cover with plastic wrap. Let dough rise until doubled in volume, about 1½ hours. Punch down dough; divide into 6 pieces. Shape each piece into ball. Roll out each on lightly floured surface to 7x4-inch oval.

Prepare barbecue (medium-high heat). Grill each flatbread until cooked through and golden, about 4 minutes per side. Transfer hot flatbreads to board. Brush with olive oil; sprinkle with za'atar. Serve warm or at room temperature.

**Available at specialty foods stores and Middle Eastern markets.*

MAKES 6

Za'atar, is a Middle Eastern spice mix made from sesame seeds, thyme, marjoram, and ground sumac.

Upside-Down Honey Cheesecakes
(page 209)

Desserts

Pies & Tarts

Fruit Desserts

Cakes

Mousses & Puddings

Frozen Desserts

Cookies & Pastries

Caramel Pudding Tart with Almond Shortbread Crust

CRUST

½ cup slivered almonds, toasted, cooled
¼ cup sugar
1 cup all purpose flour
¼ cup powdered sugar
¼ teaspoon salt
½ cup (1 stick) chilled unsalted butter, cut into ½-inch cubes
1 large egg yolk

PUDDING

2½ tablespoons cornstarch
¼ teaspoon salt
2¼ cups whole milk, divided
3 large egg yolks

1 cup sugar
⅓ cup water
3 tablespoons unsalted butter
½ teaspoon vanilla extract

TOPPING

⅔ cup sugar
⅓ cup water
1 cup slivered almonds

½ cup chilled heavy whipping cream
½ tablespoon powdered sugar
⅛ teaspoon vanilla extract
Fleur de sel*

FOR CRUST: Butter 9-inch-diameter tart pan with removable bottom. Combine almonds and ¼ cup sugar in processor; grind nuts finely. Add flour, powdered sugar, and salt; blend 5 seconds. Add butter and blend, using on/off turns, until coarse meal forms. Add egg yolk and blend until moist clumps form, about 30 seconds. Knead dough into ball. Transfer ¼ cup dough to small bowl and reserve for another use. Press remaining dough evenly onto bottom and up sides of prepared pan. Pierce bottom all over with fork. Cover pan with foil and freeze crust at least 1 hour and up to 1 day.

Preheat oven to 375°F. Bake crust uncovered until deep golden brown, checking often and pressing sides and bottom with back of fork during first 15 minutes when crust puffs or bubbles, about 20 minutes total. Cool completely.

FOR PUDDING: Place cornstarch and salt in medium bowl. Gradually add ¼ cup milk, whisking until cornstarch dissolves. Whisk in egg yolks.

Stir sugar and ⅓ cup water in heavy large saucepan over medium-high heat until sugar dissolves. Bring to boil, brushing down pan sides with wet pastry brush. Boil without stirring until syrup is deep amber, swirling pan occasionally, about 10 minutes. Add 2 cups milk (mixture will bubble). Whisk until caramel bits dissolve. Slowly whisk hot milk mixture into yolk mixture; return to same pan. Whisk until pudding thickens and boils, about 2 minutes. Remove from heat. Whisk in butter and vanilla. Transfer to crust. Chill uncovered until cold and just firm, at least 3 hours. *(Can be made 1 day ahead.)*

FOR TOPPING: Stir 2/3 cup sugar and 1/3 cup water in heavy medium skillet (do not use nonstick) over medium-high heat until sugar dissolves. Bring to boil, brushing down pan sides with wet pastry brush. Boil without stirring until syrup is medium amber color, about 7 minutes. Add almonds and stir to coat evenly with caramel. Immediately scrape coated almonds onto sheet of foil. Working quickly with 2 forks, separate almonds and spread out in single layer. Cool completely. Let almonds stand at room temperature up to 6 hours or cover and chill up to 1 day. Break into small clusters before using.

Press bottom of pan up, releasing tart. Whisk cream, powdered sugar, and vanilla in bowl until peaks form; spread over tart. Sprinkle almonds with fleur de sel. Garnish tart with clusters.

**A type of sea salt; available at some supermarkets and at specialty foods stores.*

8 TO 10 SERVINGS

Caramelized almonds and a sprinkling of fleur de sel take this tart right over the top.

Summer Peach Pie with Vanilla and Cardamom

- ⅔ cup plus 2 teaspoons sugar
- ½ vanilla bean, cut crosswise into ½-inch pieces
- 3 tablespoons unbleached all purpose flour
- 1 teaspoon (scant) ground cardamom
- 3¾ pounds firm but ripe unpeeled peaches, halved, pitted, each half cut into 4 slices (about 10 cups)

- 2 Best-Ever Pie Crust dough disks (see recipe)
- 2 tablespoons (¼ stick) unsalted butter, cut into ½-inch cubes
- Whipping cream (for glaze)

- Vanilla ice cream

Position rack in bottom third of oven and preheat to 400°F. Combine ⅔ cup sugar and vanilla bean in processor; blend until vanilla bean is very finely minced. Sift vanilla sugar through strainer into large bowl; discard any large bits in strainer. Mix flour and cardamom into vanilla sugar. Add peaches to flour-sugar mixture and toss gently to coat.

Roll out 1 pie crust disk on floured surface to 12-inch round. Transfer to 9-inch-diameter glass pie dish. Trim dough overhang to ½ inch. Spoon peach mixture into crust; dot with butter. Roll out second pie crust disk on lightly floured surface to 12-inch round. Drape dough over peach filling; trim overhang to 1½ inches. Fold top and bottom edges under, pressing together to seal. Crimp edges decoratively. Using small sharp knife, cut 2-inch-long X in center of top crust to allow steam to escape. Brush crust lightly with whipping cream; sprinkle with remaining 2 teaspoons sugar.

Place pie on rimmed baking sheet. Bake until crust is golden, peaches are tender, and juices bubble thickly through cut in top crust, about 1 hour 15 minutes. Transfer pie to rack and cool until lukewarm, about 2 hours.

Serve pie warm or at room temperature with vanilla ice cream.

8 SERVINGS

No need to peel the peaches—the peel provides great color, texture, and flavor. Just gently rub off the peach fuzz with a kitchen towel.

Best-Ever Pie Crust

- 2½ cups unbleached all purpose flour
- 1½ teaspoons sugar
- 1 teaspoon salt
- ½ cup (1 stick) chilled unsalted butter, cut into ½-inch cubes
- ½ cup chilled lard or frozen nonhydrogenated solid vegetable shortening, cut into ½-inch cubes
- 5 tablespoons (or more) ice water

Blend flour, sugar, and salt in processor. Add butter and lard; using on/off turns, blend until mixture resembles coarse meal. Transfer mixture to medium bowl. Add 5 tablespoons ice water and mix with fork until dough begins to clump together, adding more water by teaspoonfuls if dry. Gather dough together. Divide dough in half; flatten each half into disk. Wrap each disk in plastic and refrigerate at least 1 hour. *(Can be made 3 days ahead. Keep refrigerated. If necessary, soften slightly at room temperature before rolling out.)*

MAKES 2 PIE CRUSTS (ENOUGH DOUGH FOR 1 DOUBLE-CRUST PIE, 1 LATTICE-TOPPED PIE, OR 2 SINGLE-CRUST PIES)

Mango Meringue Tartlets with Coconut Crust

- 2 cups all purpose flour
- 2 cups powdered sugar, divided
- 3/4 cup (1 1/2 sticks) unsalted butter, melted, lukewarm
- 3 tablespoons sweetened flaked coconut

- 3 large ripe mangoes, peeled, pitted, sliced, divided
- 1/4 teaspoon ground allspice
- 1/4 teaspoon ground cinnamon

- 1/3 cup fresh lime juice
- 1 envelope unflavored gelatin
- 1 14-ounce can sweetened condensed milk

- 6 large egg whites
- Pinch of coarse kosher salt

- 6 fresh mint sprigs

Preheat oven to 350°F. Using fork, mix flour, 1/2 cup powdered sugar, melted butter, and coconut in medium bowl until dough forms. Divide into 6 equal pieces. Press each piece onto bottom and up sides of 4 1/2-inch-diameter tartlet pan with removable bottom. Chill crusts 30 minutes. *(Can be made 1 day ahead. Cover and chill.)*

Bake crusts until golden, pressing down with spoon if bubbles form, about 25 minutes. Cool.

Puree 2 mangoes in processor. Measure 1 3/4 cups puree (discard any remaining puree);

mix in spices. Transfer to bowl; cover and refrigerate.

Pour lime juice into small saucepan; sprinkle gelatin over. Let stand until gelatin softens, about 10 minutes. Stir over low heat just until gelatin dissolves, about 2 minutes. Remove from heat. Whisk in condensed milk, then spiced mango puree. Divide filling among cooled crusts. Chill at least 3 hours and up to 5 hours.

Using electric mixer, blend egg whites and coarse salt in large bowl. Gradually add 1½ cups powdered sugar; beat until stiff peaks form, about 5 minutes. Spoon meringue atop tartlets or pipe atop tartlets using pastry bag fitted with large star tip. Using butane torch, lightly brown meringue. (Alternatively, place tartlets in 500°F oven until meringue is golden in spots, watching carefully to prevent burning, about 3 minutes.) Garnish with remaining mango slices and mint sprigs.

MAKES 6

Brown Sugar Apple Pastries

- 1 sheet frozen puff pastry (half of 17.3-ounce package), thawed
- 6 tablespoons (¾ stick) unsalted butter, divided
- ¾ cup (packed) dark brown sugar, divided
- 1¼ teaspoons ground cinnamon, divided
- 3 8-ounce Granny Smith apples, peeled, quartered, cored, each quarter cut into 3 slices
- 1 tablespoon finely grated lemon peel
- Vanilla ice cream

Position rack in bottom third of oven and preheat to 425°F. Unfold pastry sheet on work surface. Cut into 3 strips along fold lines. Cut strips in half crosswise. Transfer rectangles to baking sheet. Blend 2 tablespoons butter, ¼ cup sugar, and ¼ teaspoon cinnamon in small bowl; spread over rectangles. Bake 10 minutes. Pierce crusts with fork to deflate; continue baking until bottoms are crisp, about 6 minutes.

Meanwhile, melt remaining 4 tablespoons butter in large skillet over medium-high heat. Add apples. Sauté until beginning to brown, about 8 minutes. Sprinkle with remaining ½ cup sugar, 1 teaspoon cinnamon, and lemon peel. Toss until syrup forms and apples are tender but still hold shape, about 5 minutes.

Transfer crusts to platter. Top each with apples; drizzle with any syrup from skillet. Serve pastries with ice cream.

MAKES 6

Dinner from the Tropics for 6

Tangerine-Ginger Caipirinhas
(page 39)

Cuban-Spiced Chicken Thighs with Chorizo and Rice
(page 72)

Escarole Salad with White Beans and Lime Vinaigrette
(page 155)

Merlot

Mango Meringue Tartlets with Coconut Crust
(opposite; pictured opposite)

Lattice-Topped Triple-Cherry Pie

1 24- to 24.7-ounce jar dark Morello cherries in light syrup
3 tablespoons cornstarch
½ cup dried tart cherries (about scant 3 ounces)
1 cinnamon stick, broken in half
1 whole nutmeg, cracked in half with mallet
1 whole star anise*
1 pound fresh Bing cherries, pitted
½ cup sugar

2 Best-Ever Pie Crust dough disks (see recipe on page 173)
Whipping cream (for glaze)

Vanilla ice cream

Strain syrup from Morello cherries into measuring cup. Combine drained Morello cherries, ¼ cup of strained Morello syrup, and cornstarch in medium bowl; stir to blend. Combine remaining strained Morello syrup, dried cherries, cinnamon, nutmeg, and star anise in heavy large saucepan. Cover and simmer over medium-low heat until cherries are plump, about 10 minutes. Uncover, increase heat to medium, and simmer until mixture bubbles thickly and is reduced to ¾ cup, stirring occasionally, about 10 minutes longer. Discard cinnamon stick, nutmeg, and star anise. Add Bing cherries and sugar and stir over medium-low heat until sugar dissolves; increase heat to medium and simmer until fresh cherries are tender when pierced with sharp knife, about 5 minutes. Add Morello cherry mixture and stir over medium heat until mixture bubbles and thickens, about 3 minutes. Transfer pie filling to medium bowl and cool completely. *(Can be made 4 hours ahead. Let stand at room temperature.)*

Position rack in bottom third of oven and preheat to 400°F. Roll out 1 pie crust disk on floured surface to 12-inch round. Transfer to 9-inch-diameter glass pie dish. Trim dough overhang to 1 inch. Spoon cooled filling into crust. Roll out second pie crust disk on lightly floured surface to 13x10-inch rectangle. Cut dough rectangle lengthwise into ¾-inch-wide strips. Arrange 5 dough strips across cherry filling in 1 direction and 5 strips in opposite direction, forming lattice and spacing evenly, weaving if desired. Brush bottom crust edge lightly with cream and press dough strips to crust to seal. Trim any overhang from dough strips. Turn dough edge of bottom crust up over dough strips, pinching gently to seal. Crimp edges decoratively. Brush edges and lattice lightly with whipping cream.

Place pie on rimmed baking sheet and bake until crust is golden brown and filling bubbles thickly, about 50 minutes. Transfer pie to rack and cool to lukewarm, about 2 hours.

Serve pie warm or at room temperature with vanilla ice cream.

**A brown, star-shaped seedpod; available in the spice section of some supermarkets and at specialty foods stores and Asian markets.*

8 SERVINGS

Mexican Chocolate Tart with Cinnamon-Spiced Pecans

PECANS

Nonstick vegetable oil spray
1 large egg white
2 tablespoons sugar
1 tablespoon golden brown sugar
1 teaspoon ground cinnamon
1/4 teaspoon salt
1/8 teaspoon cayenne pepper
1 1/2 cups pecan halves

CRUST

1 cup chocolate wafer cookie crumbs (about half of one 9-ounce package cookies, finely ground in processor)
1/4 cup sugar
1/2 teaspoon ground cinnamon
1/8 teaspoon salt
5 tablespoons unsalted butter, melted

FILLING

1 cup heavy whipping cream
4 ounces bittersweet or semisweet chocolate, chopped
1 3.1-ounce disk Mexican chocolate (such as Ibarra), chopped
1/4 cup (1/2 stick) unsalted butter, cut into 4 pieces, room temperature
2 teaspoons vanilla extract
1 teaspoon ground cinnamon
1/4 teaspoon salt

Lightly sweetened whipped cream

FOR PECANS: Preheat oven to 350°F. Spray rimmed baking sheet with nonstick spray. Whisk all ingredients except pecans in medium bowl. Stir in pecans. Spread in single layer on sheet, rounded side up. Bake until just browned and dry, about 30 minutes. Cool on sheet. Separate nuts, removing excess coating. *(Can be made 2 days ahead. Store airtight at room temperature.)*

FOR CRUST: Preheat oven to 350°F. Blend first 4 ingredients in processor. Add melted butter; process until crumbs are moistened. Press crumbs into 9-inch-diameter tart pan with removable bottom, to within 1/8 inch of top. Bake until set, about 20 minutes. Cool on rack.

FOR FILLING: Bring cream to simmer in medium saucepan. Remove from heat. Add chocolates; whisk until melted. Add butter, 1 piece at a time; whisk until smooth. Whisk in vanilla, cinnamon, and salt. Pour filling into crust. Chill until filling begins to set, about 15 to

20 minutes. Arrange nuts in concentric circles atop tart. Chill until set, about 4 hours. *(Can be made 1 day ahead. Cover loosely with foil and keep chilled.)*

Serve tart with whipped cream.

8 TO 10 SERVINGS

Wild Blueberry Pie with Almond Crumble Topping

1 Best-Ever Pie Crust dough disk (see recipe on page 173)

FILLING

¾ cup plus 2 tablespoons (or more) sugar
¼ cup cornstarch
7 cups fresh wild or regular blueberries (32 ounces) or 32 ounces frozen wild or regular blueberries (do not thaw)
2 tablespoons fresh lemon juice

TOPPING

⅔ cup unbleached all purpose flour
4 ounces marzipan or almond paste, broken into ⅓-inch pieces (about ¾ cup loosely packed)
¼ cup (½ stick) chilled unsalted butter, cut into ½-inch cubes
½ teaspoon salt

Whipped cream or ice cream

Wild blueberries are small and flavorful. They can be found fresh at farmers' markets and frozen at supermarkets and specialty foods stores. The little bit of almond in the topping amps up the flavor of the berries.

Roll out pie crust disk on floured surface to 12-inch round. Transfer to 9-inch-diameter glass pie dish. Turn crust edges under and crimp decoratively, forming crust edge ¼ inch above sides of pie dish. Refrigerate while preparing filling and topping.

FOR FILLING: Whisk ¾ cup plus 2 tablespoons sugar and cornstarch in heavy large saucepan to blend. Stir in blueberries and lemon juice. Cook over medium heat until mixture bubbles and thickens, frequently stirring gently, about 13 minutes. Chill filling until cool, about 1 hour. If more sweetness is desired, stir in sugar by tablespoonfuls.

FOR TOPPING: Combine first 4 ingredients in processor; blend until mixture begins to clump together. Transfer to bowl; chill 30 minutes.

Position rack in bottom third of oven and preheat to 400°F. Spread blueberry filling evenly in unbaked crust. Sprinkle topping evenly over. Place pie on rimmed baking sheet and bake until crust and topping are golden and filling bubbles thickly, about 50 minutes. Transfer pie to rack and cool completely. *(Can be made 8 hours ahead. Let stand at room temperature.)*

Serve pie with whipped cream or ice cream.

8 SERVINGS

Mascarpone Tart with Honey, Oranges, and Pistachios

1 refrigerated pie crust (half of 15-ounce package)

2 large navel oranges

1 8- to 8.8-ounce container chilled mascarpone cheese*
½ cup chilled heavy whipping cream
¼ cup sugar
2 tablespoons honey, divided
¼ teaspoon (generous) ground cardamom
2 tablespoons chopped pistachios

Preheat oven to 400°F. Press pie crust onto bottom and up sides of 9-inch-diameter tart pan with removable bottom; fold sides in and press to extend sides ¼ inch above rim of pan. Pierce crust all over with fork. Bake until golden brown, about 24 minutes. Cool on rack.

Meanwhile, grate enough orange peel to measure 1¼ teaspoons. Cut off remaining peel and pith from oranges. Slice oranges into thin rounds, then cut rounds crosswise in half. Place orange slices on paper towels to drain slightly.

Combine mascarpone, cream, sugar, 1 tablespoon honey, cardamom, and grated orange peel in medium bowl. Using electric mixer, beat just until blended and peaks form (do not overbeat or mixture will curdle). Spread filling evenly in cooled crust. Arrange orange slices atop tart in concentric circles; sprinkle with pistachios. Drizzle with remaining 1 tablespoon honey and serve.

**Italian cream cheese; sold at many supermarkets and Italian markets.*

8 SERVINGS

Plum Tarte Tatin

Here's a beautiful tarte Tatin with plums standing in for the apples. This can also be served with vanilla ice cream instead of the orange crème fraîche.

- 1 cup crème fraîche*
- 1 teaspoon grated orange peel
- 1 sheet frozen puff pastry (half of 17.3-ounce package), thawed

- 2¼ pounds sweet firm red plums (such as Burgundies or Satsumas), halved, pitted
- 2 tablespoons plus ⅔ cup sugar, divided
- 1 tablespoon fresh lemon juice
- 1½ teaspoons finely grated lemon peel
- ⅛ teaspoon ground nutmeg
- ½ vanilla bean, split lengthwise

- 6 tablespoons (¾ stick) unsalted butter

Whisk crème fraîche and orange peel in small bowl. Cover; chill. Roll out pastry on lightly floured surface; trim corners to create circle. Place on plate. *(Crème fraîche and crust can be prepared 1 day ahead. Cover separately and chill.)*

Preheat oven to 400°F. Mix plums, 2 tablespoons sugar, lemon juice, lemon peel, nutmeg, and seeds from vanilla bean in large bowl. Let stand 30 minutes.

Melt butter in heavy ovenproof 9-inch-diameter skillet over medium heat. Sprinkle remaining ⅔ cup sugar evenly over melted butter. Tightly arrange plums, cut side up, in concentric circles in skillet (plums will appear slightly uneven but will soften while cooking, creating even layer). Drizzle accumulated juices from bowl over top. Cook over medium heat, shaking skillet gently to prevent sticking. Continue cooking until syrup turns deep red, pressing plums slightly to form compact layer, about 35 minutes. Remove skillet from heat; cool 10 minutes.

Slide crust atop plums in skillet. Press crust edges down around plums at edge of skillet. Cut several slits to allow steam to escape. Bake until golden, about 30 minutes. Cool completely in skillet.

Rewarm in skillet set over high heat to loosen, about 3 minutes. Place large platter over skillet. Using oven mitts, hold skillet and platter together and invert, allowing tart to settle onto platter. Slowly lift off skillet. Let stand at least 30 minutes and up to 4 hours at room temperature. Serve with orange crème fraîche.

**Sold at some supermarkets and at specialty foods stores.*

6 SERVINGS

Pear and Dried-Cherry Crisp with Nutmeg-Walnut Streusel

STREUSEL

1¼ cups all purpose flour
¾ cup sugar
1½ teaspoons ground nutmeg
¼ teaspoon salt
¾ cup (1½ sticks) unsalted butter, cut into 12 pieces, room temperature
1½ cups coarsely chopped walnuts

FILLING

½ cup sugar
¼ cup (½ stick) unsalted butter, room temperature
¼ cup orange juice
2 teaspoons finely grated orange peel
1 teaspoon vanilla extract
¼ teaspoon salt
1½ cups dried tart cherries (9 ounces)

4½ pounds ripe Bosc pears, peeled, cored, cut into 1-inch cubes (about 8 cups)
Lightly sweetened whipped cream or vanilla ice cream

FRUIT

DESSERTS

FOR STREUSEL: Whisk first 4 ingredients in medium bowl. Add butter; rub in with fingertips until mixture begins to clump together. Mix in walnuts. *(Can be made 1 day ahead. Cover; chill.)*

FOR FILLING: Place first 6 ingredients in medium skillet. Stir over medium-high heat until sugar dissolves and mixture comes to boil. Add cherries; reduce heat to medium and simmer until cherries begin to soften and liquid is slightly reduced, about 5 minutes. Remove from heat and cool.

Preheat oven to 375°F. Generously butter 13x9x2-inch glass baking dish. Toss pears and dried cherry mixture in large bowl; spread in baking dish. Sprinkle streusel mixture over. Bake until bubbling and golden, about 1 hour; cool. Serve warm or at room temperature with whipped cream or ice cream.

12 SERVINGS

Nutmeg is freshest and most fragrant when ground from the whole seed with a grater (a Microplane works well). Whole nutmeg seeds can be found in the spice section of supermarkets and specialty stores.

Blackberry-Cinnamon Cobbler

- 6 cups fresh blackberries
- 1/3 cup plus 2 tablespoons sugar
- 2 tablespoons cornstarch
- 1 tablespoon fresh lemon juice
- 3/4 teaspoon ground cinnamon, divided

- 1 1/4 cups buttermilk baking mix (such as Bisquick)
- 1 1/2 teaspoons finely grated lemon peel
- 1/2 cup chilled whipping cream

- Vanilla ice cream

Preheat oven to 375°F. Toss berries, 1/3 cup sugar, cornstarch, lemon juice, and 1/2 teaspoon cinnamon in large bowl. Let stand 10 minutes, tossing occasionally. Transfer to 9-inch deep-dish glass pie plate. Bake until berries soften, about 15 minutes.

Meanwhile, combine baking mix and lemon peel in medium bowl. Add cream, tossing until soft dough forms.

Drop dough by heaping tablespoonfuls over filling. Mix 2 tablespoons sugar and 1/4 teaspoon cinnamon in cup; sprinkle cinnamon-sugar over top. Bake until filling bubbles thickly and tester inserted into biscuits comes out clean, about 25 minutes. Spoon cobbler into bowls. Top with ice cream.

6 TO 8 SERVINGS

Tropical Fruit Crepes with Vanilla Bean and Rum Butter Sauce

CREPES

1 cup whole milk
½ cup cornstarch
¼ cup all purpose flour
3 large eggs
3 tablespoons unsalted butter, melted
2 tablespoons sugar
1 tablespoon dark rum
1 teaspoon vanilla extract
¼ teaspoon coarse kosher salt

RUM BUTTER SAUCE

½ cup sugar
6 tablespoons (¾ stick) unsalted butter, room temperature
¼ teaspoon coarse kosher salt
3 tablespoons dark rum

TROPICAL FRUIT

2 tablespoons (¼ stick) unsalted butter
1 cup ¾-inch cubes peeled fresh pineapple
½ vanilla bean, split lengthwise
¼ cup sugar
¼ teaspoon coarse kosher salt
2 tablespoons fresh lime juice

1 cup ¾-inch cubes peeled seeded papaya (from about 1 large)
1 cup ¾-inch cubes peeled pitted mango (from about 1 large)

FOR CREPES: Combine all ingredients in blender. Blend until smooth. *(Crepe batter can be made 4 hours ahead. Cover and refrigerate. Reblend before using.)*

Line plate with paper towel or parchment paper. Heat 9-inch-diameter nonstick skillet with 7-inch-diameter bottom over medium heat. Add 2 tablespoons crepe batter to skillet; tilt and swirl skillet to spread batter evenly over bottom. Cook until center of crepe is cooked through and edges are lightly browned, about 1 minute. Run spatula around crepe and invert onto prepared plate. Repeat with remaining batter, placing paper towels or parchment paper between crepes. *(Can be made 1 day ahead. Cover and refrigerate.)*

FOR RUM BUTTER SAUCE: Using electric mixer, beat sugar, butter, and salt in medium bowl until fluffy, about 2 minutes. Gradually add rum and beat until well blended. *(Can be made 1 day ahead. Cover and refrigerate.)*

FOR TROPICAL FRUIT: Melt butter in large nonstick skillet over medium-high heat. Add pineapple to skillet and scrape in seeds from vanilla bean; add bean. Add sugar and salt; stir until sugar dissolves and pineapple and pan juices are lightly browned, about 4 minutes. Stir in lime juice. Remove from heat. *(Can be made 2 hours ahead. Let stand at room temperature.)*

Preheat oven to 300°F. Place crepe stack (with paper towels between crepes) on rimmed baking sheet. Cover baking sheet with foil; warm crepes in oven until heated through, about 15 minutes. Place rum butter sauce mixture in small saucepan; heat over medium heat until melted and smooth, stirring occasionally. Rewarm tropical fruit mixture over medium heat, stirring occasionally, about 3 minutes. Stir in papaya and mango.

Place 1 crepe on plate, browned side down. Spoon 2 teaspoons rum butter sauce over crepe, then fold crepe into quarters. Repeat with 2 more crepes on same plate. Spoon tropical fruit over. Repeat with remaining crepes, rum butter sauce, and tropical fruit, placing 3 crepes on each of 6 plates. Spoon any remaining rum butter sauce over crepes and serve.

6 SERVINGS

This dessert needs some last-minute assembly, so appoint a helper or line up the components to make it all go smoothly.

Cognac-Glazed Dried Apricots with Cinnamon-Spiced Yogurt

YOGURT

- 3 cups plain Greek yogurt or drained plain whole-milk yogurt
- ¾ teaspoon ground cinnamon

APRICOTS

- 1 tablespoon finely slivered orange peel (orange part only)
- 1 tablespoon butter
- 2 tablespoons sugar
- 1 pound dried pitted whole Mediterranean-style apricots (about 3 cups), halved crosswise
- 1 cup plus 2 tablespoons orange juice
- ⅓ cup Cognac or other brandy
- Toasted natural unsalted pistachios
- Slivered fresh mint

FOR YOGURT: Stir yogurt and cinnamon in medium bowl to blend. Cover and chill at least 1 hour and up to 1 day.

FOR APRICOTS: Cook orange peel in boiling water 5 minutes. Drain and reserve peel.

Melt butter in medium skillet over medium heat. Whisk in sugar. Add apricots; toss. Sauté until beginning to brown in spots, about 8 minutes. Add 1 cup orange juice and reserved orange peel. Simmer uncovered until juice is reduced to thick syrup and apricots are tender, stirring occasionally, about 8 minutes. *(Can be made 1 day ahead. Cover; chill. Bring to simmer before continuing.)*

Add Cognac to simmering apricots; ignite with long match. Let flames subside, shaking skillet occasionally. Mix in remaining 2 tablespoons orange juice and simmer 1 minute, stirring.

Spoon chilled yogurt into 6 dessert dishes. Spoon warm apricots and syrup over. Sprinkle with pistachios and mint.

6 SERVINGS

Middle Eastern Menu for 6

Zucchini Patties with Feta
(page 13)

Spicy Lamb with Charred Eggplant Puree and Pita
(page 57)

Fresh Spinach with Garlic-Yogurt Sauce
(page 147)

Rosé

Cognac-Glazed Dried Apricots with Cinnamon-Spiced Yogurt
(at left; pictured opposite)

Warm Doughnuts à la Mode with Bananas and Spiced Caramel Sauce

- 2 cinnamon crumb or glazed doughnuts
- 3 tablespoons butter
- 3 tablespoons (packed) golden brown sugar
- 2 teaspoons fresh lemon juice
- 3/4 teaspoon ground cinnamon
- 1/8 teaspoon ground nutmeg
- 1 tablespoon dark rum

- 2 small ripe bananas, peeled, cut on diagonal into 1/2-inch-thick slices
- Vanilla ice cream
- Toasted pecans

Preheat broiler. Place doughnuts on small baking sheet; set aside. Stir butter and brown sugar in heavy medium skillet over medium heat until butter is melted. Boil 1 minute, stirring occasionally. Remove from heat. Mix in lemon juice and spices, then rum; stir to blend. Cool caramel sauce 3 minutes.

Meanwhile, broil doughnuts just until hot and bubbly, watching closely to avoid burning, 1 to 2 minutes per side. Transfer doughnuts to 2 plates. Toss bananas with caramel sauce in skillet. Top doughnuts with scoop of ice cream, flattening slightly in center. Spoon bananas and caramel sauce over. Sprinkle with nuts and serve.

2 SERVINGS

Grilled Peaches with Fresh Raspberry Sauce

- 2¼ cups (lightly packed) fresh raspberries (about 13 ounces)
- 3 tablespoons water
- 3 tablespoons sugar
- 1 tablespoon fresh lemon juice

- 3 tablespoons unsalted butter
- 1½ tablespoons (packed) dark brown sugar
- 6 medium-size ripe but firm peaches, halved, pitted

Top with scoops of vanilla ice cream and a couple of shortbread cookies if you like.

Puree 2¼ cups fresh raspberries along with 3 tablespoons water in food processor until puree is smooth. Strain raspberry puree through fine-mesh strainer, pressing on solids to release as much liquid as possible; discard solids in strainer. Stir in 3 tablespoons sugar and 1 tablespoon fresh lemon juice until blended. *(Fresh raspberry sauce can be made 1 day ahead. Cover and refrigerate.)*

Prepare barbecue (medium heat). Melt butter with brown sugar in heavy small skillet over medium heat. Remove skillet from heat. Brush peach halves all over with melted butter mixture. Grill until tender, about 8 minutes, turning occasionally. Serve with sauce.

6 SERVINGS

Chocolate Strawberry Shortcakes

BISCUITS

1¼ cups all purpose flour
½ cup unsweetened cocoa powder
½ cup sugar
1 tablespoon baking powder
⅛ teaspoon salt
1 cup chilled whipping cream
½ teaspoon vanilla extract

STRAWBERRIES

2 pounds small strawberries, hulled, quartered (about 3½ cups)
8 tablespoons powdered sugar, divided
¼ cup fresh orange juice
2 tablespoons Grand Marnier or other orange liqueur
½ teaspoon finely grated orange peel
Pinch of salt

½ cup chilled whipping cream
½ cup chilled sour cream

FOR BISCUITS: Preheat oven to 400°F. Line baking sheet with parchment. Whisk first 5 ingredients in large bowl. Using electric mixer, beat cream and vanilla in medium bowl until firm peaks form. Stir cream into flour mixture until moist clumps form. Transfer mixture to lightly floured surface and knead gently until dough forms ball, about 10 turns. Pat dough out to 3/4-inch thickness. Using 3-inch cutter, cut out biscuits. Gather dough, pat out again, and cut out total of 6 biscuits. Place biscuits on prepared baking sheet.

Bake biscuits until toothpick inserted into centers comes out clean, about 15 minutes. Transfer to rack; cool.

FOR STRAWBERRIES: Stir strawberries, 6 tablespoons powdered sugar, and next 4 ingredients in medium bowl. Cover and chill at least 1 hour and up to 2 hours.

Using electric mixer, beat chilled whipping cream, sour cream, and 2 tablespoons powdered sugar until soft peaks form. Place 1 biscuit on each of 6 plates. Place large spoonful of berries with juices atop biscuits. Top with whipped cream. Pass remaining berries alongside.

6 SERVINGS

Serving the berries and cream on top is easier than splitting the biscuits, and it's a fun and pretty twist.

Blueberry and Raspberry Eton Mess

- 2 1/2 cups fresh raspberries, divided, plus more for garnish
- 2 1/2 cups fresh blueberries, divided, plus more for garnish
- 3 tablespoons sugar, divided
- 2 tablespoons crème de cassis (black-currant liqueur)

- 2 cups chilled heavy whipping cream
- 1/4 cup crème fraîche or sour cream
- 2 cups coarsely crushed purchased meringue cookies

Mix 1 cup raspberries, 1 cup blueberries, 2 tablespoons sugar, and crème de cassis in medium skillet. Coarsely crush berries with potato masher. Cook mixture over medium heat until sugar dissolves and mixture comes to simmer, stirring occasionally, about 4 minutes. Strain through sieve set over medium bowl, pressing firmly to release as much berry puree as possible; discard solids in sieve. *(Sauce can be made 2 days ahead. Cover and chill.)*

Beat cream, crème fraîche, and remaining 1 tablespoon sugar in large bowl until soft peaks form. Fold in meringue cookies, then 1 1/2 cups raspberries and 1 1/2 cups blueberries.

In each of 6 large goblets, alternate 1/2 cup cream mixture, 1 tablespoon sauce, 1/2 cup cream mixture, and 1 tablespoon sauce. Garnish each dessert with more berries. *(Can be made 3 hours ahead. Cover and chill.)*

(Taken from *Gordon Ramsay's Sunday Lunch*, published by Quadrille Publishing).

6 SERVINGS

Because the cream mixture softens the meringue cookies, this dessert shouldn't be made more than three hours ahead. This soft-crunchy sweet gets its name from Eton College near London, where the dessert originated. It's called a "mess" because the whipped cream, berries, and crushed meringue cookies are haphazardly—but deliciously—thrown together.

Ginger and Pink Grapefruit Cheesecake

CRUST

- 20 whole graham crackers, coarsely broken
- 6 tablespoons sugar
- ½ cup (1 stick) chilled unsalted butter, cut into ½-inch cubes
- 3 tablespoons finely chopped crystallized ginger

FILLING

- 1⅓ cups heavy whipping cream
- 1 1-inch-long piece fresh ginger, peeled, cut into very thin rounds
- 1 cup ginger preserves
- 1 tablespoon water

- 4 8-ounce packages cream cheese, room temperature
- 1¼ cups sugar
- 1 tablespoon ground ginger
- 2½ teaspoons vanilla extract
- ¼ teaspoon salt
- 4 large eggs

TOPPING

- 2 large pink or ruby grapefruits
- Finely chopped crystallized ginger

FOR CRUST: Position rack in center of oven and preheat to 350°F. Butter 9-inch springform pan with 2¾-inch-high sides.

Blend graham crackers and sugar in processor to coarse crumbs. Add ½ cup butter. Blend until crumbs hold together; press onto bottom and up sides of prepared pan. Bake crust until beginning to color, about 15 minutes; sprinkle with chopped ginger. Cool. Reduce oven temperature to 325°F.

Stack 3 long sheets of 18-inch-wide foil on work surface. Place cake pan in center. Fold foil snugly up sides of pan.

FOR FILLING: Bring cream and fresh ginger to simmer. Remove from heat; cover. Steep 30 minutes. Strain cream. Stir preserves and 1 tablespoon water in small saucepan over medium heat until preserves melt; strain into small bowl. Discard solids; reserve ginger jelly.

Using electric mixer, beat cream cheese in large bowl until smooth. Beat in sugar, ground ginger, vanilla, and salt. Add eggs, 1 at a time, beating well. Add 2 tablespoons ginger jelly and beat until blended. Gradually beat in strained cream. Transfer to prepared crust. Place cake pan in large roasting pan. Pour enough hot water into roasting pan to come halfway up sides of cake pan. Place cake in water bath in oven.

Bake cake until gently set, browned on top, and beginning to crack around edges, about 2 hours. Remove from water. Remove foil. Place hot cake, uncovered, in refrigerator and

chill overnight. *(Can be made 2 days ahead. Keep cake chilled. Store ginger jelly at room temperature.)*

FOR TOPPING: Line large plate with several layers of paper towels. Cut all peel and pith off grapefruits. Working over bowl, cut between membranes to release segments; place on paper towels to drain. Cover with additional paper towels, pressing to absorb excess liquid. *(Can be prepared 8 hours ahead. Chill, changing towels as needed.)*

Cut around crust. Remove pan sides. Spread 1/4 cup ginger jelly over filling; top with grapefruit, then brush with ginger jelly. Sprinkle with crystallized ginger. *(Can be made 1 hour ahead. Chill.)*

12 SERVINGS

Flourless Chocolate Cake with Toasted Hazelnuts and Brandied Cherries

BRANDIED CHERRIES

1 750-ml bottle brandy
1½ cups dried tart cherries

1 cup water
1 cup sugar

CAKE

10 ounces bittersweet or semisweet chocolate, chopped
1¼ cups (2½ sticks) unsalted butter, diced

10 large egg yolks
½ cup plus 6 tablespoons sugar
2 teaspoons vanilla extract
¼ teaspoon salt
9 large egg whites

GANACHE

8 ounces bittersweet or semisweet chocolate, chopped
1 cup heavy whipping cream

1½ cups hazelnuts, toasted, coarsely chopped

Whipped cream

FOR BRANDIED CHERRIES: Combine brandy and dried cherries in 4-cup glass container with lid. Cover and let soak at room temperature 1 week.

Bring 1 cup water and sugar to boil in medium saucepan, stirring until sugar dissolves. Remove from heat and cool syrup. Drain brandy from cherries (reserve brandy for another use). Add sugar syrup to cherries and stir to blend. Let soak at room temperature at least 2 days. *(Can be made 2 weeks ahead. Store covered at room temperature.)*

FOR CAKE: Position rack in center of oven and preheat to 350°F. Butter 10-inch-diameter springform pan with 2¾-inch-high sides. Line bottom of pan with parchment paper round. Place chocolate and 1¼ cups butter in medium metal bowl. Set bowl over saucepan of simmering water; stir until mixture is melted and smooth. Remove bowl from over water; cool to lukewarm, about 10 minutes.

Using electric mixer, beat egg yolks and ½ cup sugar in large bowl until very thick and pale yellow in color, about 5 minutes. Beat in vanilla and salt. Gently fold chocolate mixture into yolk mixture. Using clean dry beaters, beat egg whites and remaining 6 tablespoons sugar in another large bowl until peaks form.

Fold ⅓ of beaten whites into chocolate mixture. Fold in remaining whites in 2 additions. Transfer batter to prepared pan.

Bake cake until tester inserted into center comes out with moist crumbs attached, about 45 minutes (cake will be puffed and soufflé-like while baking). Cool cake in pan on rack 15 minutes (cake will fall in center). Run knife around cake sides to loosen; press edge of cake down to make level with center. Remove pan sides and cool cake completely. *(Can be made 1 day ahead. Cover and store at room temperature.)*

This over-the-top cake has impressive looks and moistness. Start the cherries ahead: They soak in brandy for a week and then in syrup for at least two days.

FOR GANACHE: Combine chocolate and cream in medium metal bowl. Set bowl over saucepan of simmering water and stir until chocolate is melted and mixture is smooth. Remove from over water; let stand until ganache cools slightly but is still pourable, about 5 minutes.

Place cooled cake on rack set over rimmed baking sheet. Pour 1/2 cup ganache over top of cake. Using offset spatula, quickly spread ganache over top and sides of cake. Freeze cake 3 minutes. Pour remaining ganache over top of cake. Working quickly but gently and grasping pan bottom and rack together, slightly tilt rack with cake from side to side, allowing ganache to flow evenly over top and down sides of cake; smooth sides with offset spatula. Press hazelnuts onto sides of cake to adhere. Chill cake until ganache is set, about 1 hour. *(Can be made 1 day ahead. Cover with cake dome and keep refrigerated. Let stand at room temperature 45 minutes before serving.)*

Cut cake into wedges. Garnish with whipped cream and spoon brandied cherries alongside.

12 SERVINGS

Apple Spice Cake with Brown Sugar Glaze

CAKE

- Nonstick vegetable oil spray
- 3 cups all purpose flour
- 1 teaspoon baking soda
- 1 teaspoon ground cinnamon
- 3/4 teaspoon salt
- 1/2 teaspoon ground nutmeg
- 1/4 teaspoon ground cloves

This moist cake keeps beautifully for a day or two after you make it.

- 1/4 teaspoon ground allspice
- 1 3/4 pounds Granny Smith apples, peeled, cored, coarsely grated
- 1 1/2 cups (3 sticks) unsalted butter, room temperature
- 1 1/2 cups sugar
- 1/2 cup (packed) golden brown sugar
- 1 teaspoon grated lemon peel
- 3 large eggs
- 1 teaspoon vanilla extract
- 1 teaspoon fresh lemon juice

GLAZE

- 1/2 cup (packed) golden brown sugar
- 1/4 cup (1/2 stick) unsalted butter
- 1/4 cup whipping cream
- 1/2 teaspoon vanilla extract
- 1/2 teaspoon fresh lemon juice
- 1/4 teaspoon salt

FOR CAKE: Position rack in center of oven and preheat to 325°F. Spray 12-cup Bundt pan with nonstick spray. Sift flour and next 6 ingredients into medium bowl. Drain grated apples in strainer. Using hands or kitchen towel, squeeze out excess liquid from apples. Measure 2 cups grated apples.

Using electric mixer, beat butter, both sugars, and lemon peel in large bowl until fluffy. Beat in eggs, 1 at a time. Mix in vanilla and lemon juice. Beat in flour mixture. Mix in grated apples. Transfer batter to prepared pan.

Bake cake until tester inserted near center comes out clean, about 1 hour. Cool in pan on rack 20 minutes.

MEANWHILE, PREPARE GLAZE: Stir all ingredients in small nonstick skillet over medium-high heat until sugar dissolves and mixture comes to boil. Reduce heat to medium; whisk until glaze is smooth, about 1 minute. Remove from heat.

Invert cake onto rack set over baking sheet. Using small skewer, pierce holes all over top of warm cake. Pour glaze over top, allowing it to be absorbed before adding more. Cool cake 30 minutes. Serve warm or at room temperature.

12 SERVINGS

Almond Praline Cake with Mascarpone Frosting and Chocolate Bark

GANACHE FILLING

1¼ cups heavy whipping cream
3 tablespoons (packed) dark brown sugar
10 ounces bittersweet or semisweet chocolate, chopped

ALMOND CAKE

1½ cups cake flour
2¼ teaspoons baking powder
¾ teaspoon salt
1 cup (packed) dark brown sugar
¾ cup (1½ sticks) unsalted butter, room temperature
3 7-ounce packages almond paste,* crumbled into 1-inch pieces
7 large eggs
1 tablespoon vanilla extract
1¾ teaspoons almond extract

ALMOND PRALINE

1 cup sugar
2 cups whole almonds, toasted

MASCARPONE FROSTING

1½ 8-ounce containers mascarpone cheese**
1½ cups chilled heavy whipping cream
3 tablespoons sugar
1 tablespoon vanilla extract

CHOCOLATE BARK

4 ounces bittersweet chocolate, chopped

FOR GANACHE FILLING: Simmer cream and sugar in medium saucepan, stirring to dissolve sugar. Add chocolate; whisk until smooth. Chill until just spreadable, about 6 hours.

FOR ALMOND CAKE: Preheat oven to 350°F. Butter three 9-inch-diameter cake pans with 1½-inch-high sides. Line bottoms with parchment paper; dust pans with flour. Whisk flour, baking powder, and salt in bowl. Using heavy-duty mixer, blend brown sugar and butter in large bowl. Beat in almond paste 1 piece at a time, then beat until smooth. Add eggs 1 at a time, beating well after each addition. Beat in extracts. Fold in dry ingredients. Divide batter among pans; smooth tops. Bake cakes until tester inserted into centers comes out clean, about 25 minutes. Cool cakes in pans on rack.

FOR ALMOND PRALINE: Line baking sheet with foil. Stir sugar and ¼ cup water in heavy medium saucepan over medium-low heat until sugar dissolves. Increase heat; boil without stirring until deep amber, swirling pan and brushing down sides with wet pastry brush occasionally. Mix in nuts. Pour onto foil; cool. Peel foil off praline. Chop praline coarsely. *(Praline can be made 1 day ahead; store airtight at room temperature.)*

FOR MASCARPONE FROSTING: Beat all ingredients in large bowl just to soft peaks (do not overbeat or mixture will curdle).

Run knife around pan sides to loosen cakes. Turn cakes out; peel off paper. Place 1 cake layer on platter. Spread half of ganache over; sprinkle with 1/4 cup praline. Top with second cake layer. Spread remaining ganache over; sprinkle with 1/4 cup praline. Top with third cake layer. Spread frosting over top and sides of cake. *(Cake can be made 1 day ahead. Cover with cake dome and chill. Store remaining praline airtight at room temperature.)*

FOR CHOCOLATE BARK: Line baking sheet with foil. Melt chocolate in small bowl set over saucepan of simmering water. Stir until smooth. Remove from over water. Drizzle all but 1 tablespoon chocolate over foil in thick (about 1-inch-wide) zigzag lines (chocolate will pool in spots). Sprinkle 3 tablespoons praline over chocolate; chill bark until firm, about 1 hour.

Press praline around bottom 2 inches of cake; sprinkle more atop. Peel foil off bark; break into pieces. Press edges into frosting atop cake. Remelt 1 tablespoon chocolate over simmering water, stirring often. Using spoon, drizzle chocolate over cake. Chill up to 4 hours. Serve cold or at room temperature.

**Available in the baking section of most supermarkets and at specialty foods stores.*
***Italian cream cheese; sold at many supermarkets and at Italian markets.*

12 SERVINGS

Chocolate-Honey Dome Cake with Chocolate-Honey Glaze

CAKE

- Nonstick vegetable oil spray
- 2¼ cups all purpose flour
- ¼ cup unsweetened cocoa powder
- 1 teaspoon baking soda
- ½ teaspoon salt
- ¾ cup sugar
- ½ cup honey
- 2 large eggs
- 1 teaspoon vanilla extract
- ¾ cup vegetable oil
- 1½ cups buttermilk

CREAM FILLING

- 1 tablespoon water
- 1 teaspoon unflavored gelatin
- 1¼ cups heavy whipping cream, divided
- ½ cup sour cream
- 3 tablespoons honey
- ½ cup finely grated bittersweet chocolate (about 1 ounce)

CHOCOLATE-HONEY GLAZE

- 10 ounces bittersweet chocolate, chopped
- 1 cup heavy whipping cream
- ½ cup honey
- 1 cup pecans, toasted, chopped

FOR CAKE: Preheat oven to 350°F. Spray 9-inch-diameter cake pan with 2-inch-high sides with nonstick spray. Line bottom with parchment round. Whisk flour, cocoa powder, baking soda, and salt in medium bowl. Whisk sugar, honey, eggs, and vanilla in large bowl to blend. Whisk in oil, then half of dry ingredients. Whisk in buttermilk, then remaining dry ingredients. Pour into prepared pan.

Bake cake until tester inserted into center comes out clean, about 55 minutes (cake will dome). Cool 10 minutes. Invert onto rack; remove parchment. Turn over; cool cake completely on rack. *(Can be made 1 day ahead. Store airtight at room temperature.)*

FOR CREAM FILLING: Cut cake in half horizontally. Place bottom half of cake on cardboard round, tart pan bottom, or springform pan bottom. Place 1 tablespoon water in small bowl. Sprinkle gelatin over. Let stand 10 minutes to soften gelatin. Bring ¼ cup whipping cream to boil in small saucepan. Remove from heat and stir in gelatin mixture. Cool filling

The unusual duo of honey and chocolate is a winner in this layer cake. It needs to set up overnight, so begin a day ahead.

to room temperature, stirring often, about 5 minutes.

Meanwhile, using electric mixer, beat remaining 1 cup cream, sour cream, and honey in medium bowl until peaks form. Beat gelatin mixture, then grated chocolate into whipped cream mixture. Immediately spread filling over bottom half of cake, leaving ½-inch border at edges. Place top half of cake atop filling, pressing gently to spread filling just to edge of cake. Cover and chill cake overnight.

FOR CHOCOLATE-HONEY GLAZE: Place chocolate in large measuring cup. Bring cream and honey to boil in heavy small saucepan, stirring to blend. Pour hot cream mixture over chocolate in cup; stir until smooth. Let cool 5 minutes.

Place rack on rimmed baking sheet. Transfer cake to rack. Pour glaze over cake, allowing glaze to drip down sides. Use spatula to spread glaze over sides. Pat nuts onto sides of cake. Chill 1 hour to set glaze. *(Can be made 1 day ahead. Keep refrigerated.)*

12 SERVINGS

Ouzo-Scented Almond, Yogurt, and Olive Oil Cake

2 cups whole almonds, divided
3/4 cup ouzo (unsweetened anise liqueur) or Pernod

3 1/2 cups unbleached all purpose flour
1 3/4 teaspoons ground anise*
1 tablespoon baking powder
1/2 teaspoon fine sea salt

4 large eggs, separated
1 1/2 cups plus 2 tablespoons sugar
1 cup extra-light olive oil
1 cup plus 2 tablespoons plain whole-milk yogurt

Position rack in center of oven and preheat to 375°F. Brush two 8 1/2x4 1/2x2 1/2-inch metal loaf pans with olive oil. Line pan bottoms with parchment paper; brush parchment with olive oil. Spread 1 1/2 cups almonds on rimmed baking sheet; toast in oven 10 minutes. Cool. Transfer to processor and coarsely grind (some small almond pieces should remain); set aside. Finely chop 1/2 cup untoasted almonds in processor. Boil ouzo in small saucepan until reduced to 1/2 cup, about 2 minutes. Cool.

Sprinkle 1 1/2 tablespoons finely chopped untoasted almonds over bottom of each pan. Whisk flour, ground star anise, baking powder, sea salt, and ground toasted almonds in large bowl.

Using electric mixer, beat egg yolks and 1 1/2 cups sugar in medium bowl until well blended (mixture will look grainy at first). Add 1 cup light olive oil; beat 1 minute. Add ouzo and yogurt and beat until well blended, about 30 seconds. Gradually add flour mixture to yolk mixture, beating just until incorporated (batter will be thick).

Using dry clean beaters, beat egg whites in large bowl until stiff but not dry. Fold 1/3 of whites into batter to lighten. Fold in remaining whites in 2 additions. Divide batter between prepared pans (about 3 1/2 cups for each). Sprinkle each with remaining finely chopped untoasted almonds, dividing equally. Sprinkle each with 1 tablespoon sugar.

Bake cakes until golden brown and tester inserted into centers comes out clean, about 1 hour 5 minutes. Cool cakes in pans on rack 15 minutes. Turn cakes out onto rack and cool completely. *(Can be made 1 day ahead. Wrap in foil and store at room temperature.)*

MAKES TWO 8-INCH LOAVES

Mediterranean Dinner for 6

Hummus with Crudités

Striped Bass with Saffron Vegetables and Spiced Broccoli Rabe
(page 98)

Couscous

Pinot Noir

Ouzo-Scented Almond, Yogurt, and Olive Oil Cake
(at left; pictured opposite)

Hazelnut Gâteau Breton

- 1¼ cups sugar
- ½ whole vanilla bean, coarsely chopped

- ½ cup hazelnuts, lightly toasted, husked
- 6 large egg yolks (preferably organic)
- 1 cup (2 sticks) salted butter, melted
- 2 cups unbleached all purpose flour

- 1 large egg yolk beaten with 2 teaspoons water (for glaze)

Whole strawberries with stems attached or warm strawberry jam

Blend sugar and vanilla bean in processor until bean is finely ground. Store in covered container 2 days.

Position rack in center of oven and preheat to 325°F. Butter and flour 9-inch-diameter springform pan. Strain vanilla sugar through fine sieve. Combine 2 tablespoons vanilla sugar and hazelnuts in processor; blend until nuts are finely ground but not pasty. Combine 6 egg yolks and remaining 1 cup plus 2 tablespoons vanilla sugar in large bowl; whisk until well blended and slightly thicker, about 2 minutes (do not use electric mixer). Whisk in hazelnut mixture. Gradually whisk in melted butter. Sift flour over batter; stir just until blended (batter will be thick; do not overmix or cake may be tough).

Transfer batter to prepared pan; smooth top with offset spatula (layer will be thin). Brush top generously with egg glaze. Using back of tines of fork, deeply mark crisscross pattern atop cake, marking 3 times across in 1 direction and 3 times in opposite direction. Bake cake until deep golden on top and tester inserted into center comes out clean, about 1 hour. Cool in pan on rack 15 minutes, then remove pan sides and cool cake completely.

(Can be made 1 day ahead. Wrap in foil and store at room temperature.)

Cut cake into wedges and serve with whole strawberries or with warm strawberry jam.

12 SERVINGS

Upside-Down Honey Cheesecakes

These crustless individual cheesecakes have a gooey, honeyed topping.

- 1 cup sugar
- 1/3 cup honey
- 1/4 cup (1/2 stick) unsalted butter
- 1/3 cup water

- 3 8-ounce packages cream cheese, room temperature
- 2/3 cup (packed) golden brown sugar
- 1 cup sour cream
- 2 teaspoons fresh lemon juice
- 2 teaspoons vanilla extract
- 4 large eggs, room temperature

Assorted fresh berries (for garnish)
Mint sprigs

Preheat oven to 300°F. Butter twelve 3/4-cup ramekins or custard cups. Place 1 cup sugar, honey, and butter in heavy medium saucepan. Stir over medium heat until butter melts and mixture is blended. Increase heat to medium-high and bring to boil. Whisk until mixture darkens slightly and candy thermometer registers 300°F, about 5 minutes. Remove from heat; add 1/3 cup water (mixture will bubble vigorously); whisk to blend. Divide topping among ramekins (about 2 tablespoonfuls for each). Divide ramekins between 2 roasting pans and chill while preparing filling.

Using on/off turns, blend cream cheese and brown sugar in processor, scraping bowl occasionally. Add sour cream, lemon juice, and vanilla; process until smooth. Add eggs 1 at a time, processing just to blend between additions. Divide filling among ramekins. Add enough hot water to pans to come halfway up sides of ramekins.

Bake cheesecakes until set, about 35 minutes. Remove from roasting pans and chill until firm, about 1 hour. *(Can be made 2 days ahead. Cover and keep chilled.)*

Run thin knife around sides of ramekins. Invert onto plates, scooping any remaining topping from ramekins over cheesecakes. Garnish with berries and mint.

12 SERVINGS

Blender Chocolate Mousse with Lemon Cream

1 cup bittersweet or semisweet chocolate chips
3/4 cup water
3 tablespoons sugar, divided
1/4 teaspoon instant espresso powder or instant coffee powder
3 large egg whites

1/3 cup chilled whipping cream
1 teaspoon fresh lemon juice
1/2 teaspoon grated lemon peel

Place chocolate in blender. Bring 3/4 cup water, 2 tablespoons sugar, and espresso powder to simmer in medium saucepan, stirring to dissolve sugar. Pour over chocolate. Cover tightly; blend 5 seconds. Add egg whites. Cover tightly; blend on high 1 minute. Pour into 4 small bowls. Chill until firm, about 2 hours.

Whisk cream, lemon juice, peel, and 1 tablespoon sugar in small bowl to very soft peaks. Spoon over mousse; serve.

4 SERVINGS

Panna Cotta Parfaits with Raspberry Compote

1/4 cup water
1 1/4 teaspoons unflavored gelatin

2 cups whipping cream, divided
3/4 cup sugar, divided
1/4 cup sour cream
1 teaspoon vanilla extract

2 1/2-pint containers raspberries

1 1/2 teaspoons balsamic vinegar

Place water in very small saucepan; sprinkle gelatin over. Let stand until gelatin softens, about 10 minutes.

Combine 1/2 cup cream and 1/2 cup sugar in medium saucepan. Stir over low heat until sugar dissolves. Pour into large bowl. Whisk in 1 1/2 cups cream, then sour cream and vanilla just until mixed.

Stir gelatin mixture over very low heat until gelatin dissolves; whisk into cream mixture. Place 1 berry in each of 6 Champagne flutes. Add cream mixture, dividing evenly. Chill until panna cotta sets, about 3 hours.

Toss remaining berries, 1/4 cup sugar, and vinegar in bowl; spoon over parfaits.

MAKES 6

Rhubarb Sponge Pudding

- 1⅓ pounds rhubarb, cut into 1-inch lengths (about 5 cups)
- ⅓ cup (packed) golden brown sugar
- 2 tablespoons water

- 1 cup plus 2 tablespoons all purpose flour
- 1½ teaspoons baking powder
- ½ cup sugar
- 7 tablespoons butter, room temperature
- 2 large eggs
- 6½ tablespoons whole milk

Softly whipped cream

Preheat oven to 375°F. Butter 11x7x2-inch baking dish. Place rhubarb pieces in baking dish in even layer. Scatter brown sugar over and sprinkle with 2 tablespoons water.

Whisk flour and baking powder in small bowl to blend. Using electric mixer, beat sugar and butter in large bowl until fluffy, about 3 minutes. Add eggs one at a time, beating well between additions. Fold in flour mixture in 3 additions alternately with milk in 2 additions, mixing just to blend after each addition. Spoon over rhubarb, smoothing top to cover.

Bake dessert until top is golden brown and toothpick inserted into center comes out clean, about 40 minutes. Cool at least 30 minutes and up to 1 hour. Serve rhubarb pudding warm with softly whipped cream.

8 SERVINGS

Lime and Lemon Pudding

- 2 1/4 cups whipping cream
- 3/4 cup plus 1 teaspoon sugar
- 3 tablespoons fresh lemon juice
- 2 tablespoons fresh lime juice

- 1 teaspoon grated lemon peel
- 1 teaspoon grated lime peel

Bring cream and 3/4 cup sugar to boil over medium-high heat, stirring until sugar dissolves. Boil 3 minutes, stirring constantly, adjusting heat as needed to prevent mixture from boiling over. Remove from heat. Stir in lemon juice and lime juice and cool 10 minutes. Stir mixture again and divide among six 1/2-cup ramekins or custard cups. Cover and chill puddings until set, at least 4 hours or overnight.

Mix remaining 1 teaspoon sugar, lemon peel, and lime peel in small bowl. Sprinkle atop puddings and serve.

6 SERVINGS

Lunch from the Pub for 4

Corn and Bell Pepper Chowder
(page 24)

Fish and Chips with Tarragon-Malt Vinegar Mayonnaise
(page 91)

Ale

Lime and Lemon Pudding
(at left; pictured at left)

Lime and Lemon Tea Cakes
(page 228)

Chocolate Bread Pudding with Walnuts and Chocolate Chips

- 4 cups 1-inch cubes egg bread with crust (about 6 ounces)
- 1¼ cups semisweet or bittersweet chocolate chips, divided
- ½ cup walnuts, toasted, broken into ½-inch pieces
- 1 cup heavy whipping cream, divided
- 1 cup half and half, divided
- 5 tablespoons unsweetened cocoa powder
- 4 large eggs
- 1 large egg yolk
- ½ cup sugar

Lightly sweetened whipped cream

Toss bread cubes, ½ cup chocolate chips, and toasted walnuts in large bowl to blend. Whisk ½ cup cream, ½ cup half and half, and cocoa in heavy medium saucepan to blend. Add remaining ¾ cup chocolate chips; stir over low heat until melted and smooth. Gradually whisk in remaining ½ cup cream and ½ cup half and half. Whisk eggs, egg yolk, and sugar in medium bowl to blend. Whisk in chocolate-cream mixture. Stir into bread mixture. Let stand 1 hour for bread to absorb some of custard.

Preheat oven to 325°F. Butter six 1- to 1¼-cup ramekins. Divide pudding mixture among ramekins. Bake puddings until set in centers, about 40 minutes.

Top warm puddings with whipped cream and serve.

MAKES 6

Raspberry-Nectarine Parfaits with Warm Peach Sabayon

The light custard is quick to make, but it has to be prepared just before it's served.

- 1 pound nectarines (about 4 medium), halved, pitted, thinly sliced
- 2½ cups fresh raspberries, divided
- ½ cup sugar, divided

- 4 large egg yolks
- ⅓ cup canned peach nectar
- ¼ cup peach liqueur
- Pinch of salt

- Toasted sliced almonds (optional)

Toss nectarines, 2 cups raspberries, and ¼ cup sugar in medium bowl. Let stand until juices form, about 5 minutes.

Whisk egg yolks, nectar, liqueur, salt, and ¼ cup sugar in large metal bowl to blend. Place bowl over saucepan of boiling water; whisk until mixture is thick and thermometer inserted into center registers at least 160°F, about 6 minutes.

Divide fruit mixture among 4 large glasses. Spoon warm sabayon over. Garnish with remaining berries and sliced almonds, if desired.

4 SERVINGS

Quick Chocolate-Cinnamon Mousse with Cherries

CHERRIES

8 ounces fresh Bing cherries, pitted
⅓ cup black cherry preserves or other cherry preserves
⅓ cup ruby Port or cherry juice

MOUSSE

1¼ cups chilled heavy whipping cream, divided
⅛ teaspoon (generous) ground cinnamon
4 ounces bittersweet or semisweet chocolate, chopped

FOR CHERRIES: Combine cherries, cherry preserves, and Port in heavy small saucepan. Bring to boil over high heat. Reduce heat to medium and boil until juices thicken to syrup consistency, stirring frequently, about 10 minutes. Remove from heat. Transfer to small bowl and chill until cold, about 3 hours. *(Can be made 1 day ahead. Cover and keep chilled.)*

FOR MOUSSE: Combine ¼ cup cream and cinnamon in small saucepan; bring to boil. Remove from heat. Add chocolate and whisk until melted and smooth. Transfer chocolate mixture to large bowl. Using electric mixer, beat remaining 1 cup cream in medium bowl until soft peaks form. Fold ¼ of whipped cream into lukewarm chocolate mixture. Fold remaining whipped cream into chocolate mixture in 3 additions just until incorporated. Divide mousse among 4 glasses or bowls. Chill until set, about 4 hours. *(Can be made 1 day ahead. Cover; keep chilled.)*

Spoon cherries with syrup atop mousse and serve.

4 SERVINGS

Strawberry and Blueberry Summer Pudding

A simple, traditional British dessert that combines fresh berries, buttered bread, and a little sugar—and it couldn't be more delicious. Start the recipe at least 12 hours ahead.

2 pounds strawberries, hulled, sliced (about 2¾ cups)
6 tablespoons sugar, divided
Pinch of salt
1 pound blueberries (generous 3 cups)

4 tablespoons (½ stick) unsalted butter, room temperature
12 slices firm-textured white bread (such as Pepperidge Farm Original), crusts removed

2 cups chilled whipping cream
¼ cup powdered sugar
1 teaspoon vanilla extract

Place strawberries, 2 tablespoons sugar, and salt in large bowl. Mash to coarse puree. Stir blueberries and 4 tablespoons sugar in large saucepan over medium heat until sugar dissolves and berries release juices, about 7 minutes. Increase heat; boil until mixture thickens slightly, stirring often, about 5 minutes. Remove from heat; add strawberry mixture.

Line 6-cup bowl with 3 sheets plastic wrap, leaving 6-inch overhang. Generously butter 1 side of bread slices. Line bowl with bread, buttered side up, cutting pieces to cover bowl. Pour berry mixture into bread-lined bowl. Top with remaining bread, buttered side down, cutting pieces to cover completely. Fold plastic wrap over bread. Place plate slightly smaller than top of bowl atop pudding. Weigh down plate with 4 pounds of canned goods or dried beans and chill at least 12 hours and up to 36 hours.

Beat cream, powdered sugar, and vanilla in large bowl until peaks form. Remove weights and plate from pudding. Open plastic wrap. Place large plate atop bowl and invert pudding. Remove bowl, then plastic. Spoon pudding onto plates. Serve with whipped cream.

8 SERVINGS

Pizzelle S'mores with Ice Cream and Chocolate Sauce

SAUCE

1⅓ cups whipping cream
8 ounces bittersweet or semisweet chocolate, chopped

PIZZELLE

1¾ cups all purpose flour
2 teaspoons baking powder
Pinch of salt
¾ cup sugar
½ cup (1 stick) unsalted butter, room temperature
2 teaspoons anise extract
1 teaspoon vanilla extract
3 large eggs
½ cup whole milk

Nonstick vegetable oil spray

24 large marshmallows
Chocolate ice cream

FOR SAUCE: Bring cream to simmer in medium saucepan. Remove from heat. Add chocolate and whisk until smooth. *(Can be made 1 week ahead. Cover; refrigerate. Rewarm until just pourable before using.)*

FOR PIZZELLE: Whisk first 3 ingredients in small bowl. Using electric mixer, beat sugar and butter in medium bowl until blended. Beat in extracts, then eggs, 1 at a time. Beat in dry ingredients in 3 additions, alternately with milk in 2 additions. Let rest 15 minutes.

Preheat waffle iron to medium heat (follow manufacturer's instructions for pizzelle iron). Spray with nonstick spray. Drop 1 generous tablespoon batter into each of 4 squares on hot waffle iron. Close cover and cook until pizzelle are golden and cooked through, about 2 minutes. Transfer to rack. Repeat, making total of at least 24 pizzelle waffles, each about 3½ inches in diameter. *(Can be made 6 hours ahead. Let stand at room temperature. Rewarm on baking sheet in 350°F oven 5 minutes before using.)*

Working with 4 at a time, place 2 marshmallows on 1 warm pizzelle. Cover with another warm pizzelle and press to compact. Arrange S'mores on plates; top with chocolate ice cream and warm chocolate sauce.

MAKES 12

Five-Minute Vanilla Ice Cream Pie with Warm Berry Compote

- 1 quart vanilla ice cream, slightly softened
- 1 9-inch purchased chocolate-cookie pie crust or graham-cracker pie crust
- 1/3 cup purchased chocolate syrup (in squirt bottle)
- 2 tablespoons toasted almonds, chopped

- 2 6-ounce containers blueberries
- 2 6-ounce containers raspberries
- 2 6-ounce containers blackberries
- 2 tablespoons water
- 2 tablespoons brown sugar

Spoon ice cream into crust; smooth top. Squeeze chocolate sauce in straight lines over pie, spacing 1/2 inch apart. Draw tip of knife through chocolate lines, forming chevron pattern. Sprinkle with almonds; freeze until firm. *(Can be made 1 day ahead; keep frozen. Let pie soften slightly before serving.)*

Just before serving, bring all berries, 2 tablespoons water, and brown sugar to simmer in medium saucepan over medium-high heat. Cook until sauce thickens, stirring gently, about 4 minutes; remove from heat. Cut pie into wedges; place on plates. Spoon warm sauce over.

6 SERVINGS

Fresh Strawberry Sorbet

- 1 cup water
- 1 cup sugar
- 4 cups quartered hulled fresh strawberries (about 18 ounces) plus additional whole strawberries for garnish
- 3 tablespoons fresh lime juice

The perfect ending to a springtime brunch. Use the best strawberries you can find for great berry flavor. Partner with your favorite shortbread cookies.

Combine 1 cup water and sugar in medium saucepan. Stir over medium-high heat until sugar dissolves and mixture comes to boil. Reduce heat and simmer 5 minutes. Transfer to bowl and chill until cold.

Puree quartered strawberries in processor until smooth. Add lime juice and sugar syrup; process until blended. Chill mixture until cold, about 1 hour.

Transfer strawberry mixture to ice cream maker and process according to manufacturer's instructions. Spoon sorbet into container; cover and freeze until firm, about 4 hours. *(Can be made 3 days ahead.)*

Scoop sorbet into glasses or bowls; garnish with strawberries.

6 SERVINGS

Chocolate Cookie Ice Cream Sandwiches

- 2 cups all purpose flour
- 1/2 cup unsweetened cocoa powder
- 1 teaspoon baking soda
- 1/2 teaspoon salt
- 1 cup (2 sticks) unsalted butter, room temperature
- 1 cup sugar
- 1 cup (packed) golden brown sugar
- 2 large eggs
- 1 teaspoon vanilla extract
- 1 12-ounce package semisweet chocolate chips (about 2 cups)

- 3 pints ice cream (such as strawberry, coffee, mint-chip, and/or banana), softened slightly, if necessary
- Assorted decorations (such as sprinkles and tiny candies)

Preheat oven to 350°F. Line 2 large rimmed baking sheets with parchment paper. Sift flour, cocoa, baking soda, and salt into medium bowl. Using electric mixer, beat butter in large bowl until fluffy. Gradually beat in both sugars. Beat in eggs, 1 at a time, then vanilla and dry ingredients. Stir in chips.

For each cookie, drop 2 heaping tablespoonfuls batter onto prepared sheets, spacing 2 inches apart. Flatten slightly. Bake cookies until dry-looking but slightly soft to touch, about 20 minutes. Cool on sheets. Layer in container between sheets of waxed paper. Cover; freeze. *(Can be made 2 days ahead. Keep frozen.)*

Place 1 cookie, flat side up, on work surface. Top with 1/3 cup ice cream; flatten slightly. Top with another cookie, flat side down. Roll edges in desired decorations. Form more sandwiches. Freeze until firm, if desired. *(Can be assembled 3 days ahead. Wrap tightly and keep frozen.)*

MAKES ABOUT 14 SANDWICHES

Peach Sundaes with Caramel

PEACH SAUCE

1 tablespoon fresh lime juice
4 8- to 9-ounce peaches, peeled, halved, pitted, thinly sliced

1 cup water
½ cup sugar
½ teaspoon ground cardamom

CARAMEL SAUCE

2 cups sugar
½ cup water
1 cup heavy whipping cream

1 pint vanilla ice cream
1 pint peach ice cream
1 ½-pint blackberries

FOR PEACH SAUCE: Place lime juice in medium bowl. Add peaches and toss to coat.

Stir 1 cup water, sugar, and cardamom in medium saucepan over medium heat until sugar dissolves. Increase heat; boil until syrup is reduced to generous ⅓ cup, stirring often, about 8 minutes. Mix hot syrup into peaches. Cool. *(Can be made 1 day ahead. Cover; chill.)*

FOR CARAMEL SAUCE: Combine sugar and ½ cup water in heavy deep medium saucepan. Stir over medium heat until sugar dissolves. Increase heat and bring syrup to boil, occasionally brushing down sides of pan with wet pastry brush. Boil without stirring until syrup turns dark amber color, swirling pan occasionally, about 13 minutes. Remove from heat and add cream (mixture will bubble up). Stir caramel until smooth. *(Caramel sauce can be made 3 days ahead. Transfer to microwave-safe bowl. Cool. Cover and chill. Rewarm in microwave in 15-second intervals before using.)*

Scoop ice cream into bowls, layering with each sauce. Top with berries and serve.

4 SERVINGS

Frozen Meyer Lemon Cream with Blackberry Sauce

- ½ cup plus 2 tablespoons sugar
- 5 tablespoons plus 1½ teaspoons strained fresh Meyer lemon juice
- 3 large egg yolks
- 1 tablespoon light corn syrup

- 1 cup chilled heavy whipping cream
- 1¾ teaspoons finely grated Meyer lemon peel, divided

- 1 cup frozen unsweetened blackberries, thawed

Whisk ½ cup sugar, 5 tablespoons lemon juice, egg yolks, and corn syrup in small metal bowl to blend. Set bowl over saucepan of boiling water; whisk until mixture is thick and fluffy and thermometer inserted into mixture registers 180°F, about 3 minutes. Place bowl with yolk mixture over larger bowl filled with ice and water until mixture is cool, stirring occasionally, about 8 minutes.

Meanwhile, using electric mixer, beat cream, 1½ teaspoons lemon peel, and 1 tablespoon sugar in medium bowl until stiff peaks form. Fold cooled yolk mixture into cream in 3 additions. Cover and freeze until firm, about 4 hours.

Mix berries and any accumulated juices, 1 tablespoon sugar, 1½ teaspoons lemon juice, and ¼ teaspoon lemon peel in small bowl; let stand 10 minutes. Coarsely mash half of berries in bowl. Scoop lemon cream into bowls. Top each with berry sauce and serve.

6 SERVINGS

Lime Granita

- 2 cups water
- 1 cup sugar
- ½ cup fresh lime juice

Bring 2 cups water and 1 cup sugar to boil in medium saucepan, stirring until sugar dissolves. Reduce heat to medium and simmer 5 minutes. Cool syrup. Stir in lime juice. Transfer to 11x7x2-inch glass baking dish. Cover and place in freezer. Stir every 45 minutes until frozen, about 3 hours. *(Can be made 2 days ahead. Cover and keep frozen.)* Using fork, scrape granita to loosen and serve.

6 SERVINGS

Spring Dinner for 6

Grilled Prosciutto-Wrapped Asparagus

Grilled Butterflied Leg of Lamb

Potato-Onion Gratin
(page 142)

Pea Salad with Radishes and Feta Cheese
(page 150)

Zinfandel

Frozen Meyer Lemon Cream with Blackberry Sauce
(at left; pictured opposite)

Chocolate-Caramel Slice

CRUST

1 cup all purpose flour
¼ cup (packed) golden brown sugar
2 teaspoons cornstarch
¼ teaspoon salt
½ cup (1 stick) chilled unsalted butter, cut into ½-inch cubes
1 tablespoon ice water
1 large egg yolk

TOPPINGS

1 14-ounce can sweetened condensed milk
½ cup (packed) golden brown sugar
6 tablespoons (¾ stick) unsalted butter, diced
2 tablespoons golden syrup (such as Lyle's Golden Syrup) or dark corn syrup
1 teaspoon vanilla extract

6 ounces bittersweet or semisweet chocolate, chopped
3 tablespoons whipping cream
Flaked sea salt (such as Maldon)

FOR CRUST: Preheat oven to 350°F. Butter 11x7x2-inch metal baking pan. Blend first 4 ingredients in processor. Add butter. Using on/off turns, blend until coarse meal forms. Add 1 tablespoon ice water and egg yolk. Blend until moist clumps form. Press dough onto bottom of pan; pierce all over with fork. Bake until golden, piercing if crust bubbles, about 20 minutes. Cool completely.

FOR TOPPINGS: Whisk first 5 ingredients in medium saucepan over medium heat until sugar dissolves, butter melts, and mixture comes to boil. Attach candy thermometer to side of pan. Boil gently until caramel is thick and temperature registers 225°F, whisking constantly, about 6 minutes. Pour caramel evenly over crust; cool 15 minutes to set.

Meanwhile, melt chocolate with cream in microwave in 15-second intervals, stirring occasionally. Spread chocolate over warm caramel; sprinkle with sea salt. Refrigerate until chocolate is set, at least 1 hour. *(Can be made 3 days ahead. Cover and keep refrigerated.)*

Cut dessert lengthwise into 4 strips. Cut each strip crosswise into 5 or 6 slices. Transfer to platter and serve.

MAKES 20 TO 24

Fig and Rum Squares

- 2 cups all purpose flour
- 1 cup (2 sticks) chilled unsalted butter, diced
- 1 cup (packed) golden brown sugar, divided
- 1/4 teaspoon salt
- 4 tablespoons dark rum, divided

- 1 9-ounce package dried black Mission figs, stemmed
- 1/3 cup orange juice
- 1 tablespoon grated orange peel
- 1 teaspoon ground cinnamon
- 3/4 cup sliced almonds

Preheat oven to 350°F. Blend flour, butter, 1/2 cup sugar, and salt in processor until coarse meal forms. Add 1 tablespoon rum; blend until moist dough forms. Measure 1 cup dough; reserve for topping. Press remaining dough into 11 1/2x7 1/2-inch metal baking pan.

Blend figs, orange juice, orange peel, cinnamon, 1/2 cup sugar, and 3 tablespoons rum in processor to coarse paste. Spread filling over crust. Mix sliced almonds into reserved 1 cup dough. Drop topping by small clumps onto filling. Bake until golden, about 35 minutes. Cool completely in pan. Cut lengthwise into 3 strips, then cut each strip crosswise into 6 pieces.

MAKES 18

Dessert Buffet for 24

Apricot-Almond Tart
(double recipe; page 172)

Ginger and Pink Grapefruit Cheesecake
(double recipe; page 196)

Chocolate-Honey Dome Cake with Chocolate-Honey Glaze
(double recipe; page 204)

Fig and Rum Squares
(double recipe; at left)

Pistachio Shortbread
(page 231)

Chocolate-Dipped Strawberries

Chocolate Truffles

Champagne

Coffee and *Tea*

Chocolate-Orange Cookie Stacks

1 cup chilled heavy whipping cream
⅔ cup frozen orange juice concentrate, partially thawed

40 chocolate wafer cookies (about one 9-ounce package)

Finely grated orange peel

Using electric mixer, beat whipping cream and orange juice concentrate in medium bowl until stiff peaks form.

Place 8 cookies on rimmed baking sheet, spacing apart. Spoon about 1 level tablespoon whipped orange cream atop each cookie, then top each with second cookie and another tablespoon cream. Repeat 2 more times with cookies and cream, creating 8 stacks of 4 cookies with 4 layers of orange cream. Top each stack with fifth cookie. Transfer remaining orange cream to small bowl; cover and chill cream. Cover and chill stacks at least 6 hours or overnight (cookies will soften).

Carefully transfer 1 stack to each of 8 plates. Rewhisk reserved orange cream, if necessary, until stiff peaks form. Spoon dollop of orange cream atop each stack, sprinkle with grated orange peel, and serve.

8 SERVINGS

Lime and Lemon Tea Cakes

14 tablespoons butter, melted, divided
¾ cup slivered almonds (about 4 ounces)
½ cup all purpose flour
6 large egg whites
2 cups powdered sugar plus additional for sprinkling
1 tablespoon finely grated lemon peel
1 tablespoon finely grated lime peel

Preheat oven to 400°F. Brush twelve ⅓-cup muffin cups with 1 tablespoon melted butter. Place almonds and flour in processor and pulse until almonds are finely ground. Beat egg whites in large bowl until frothy. Sift 2 cups sugar over egg whites. Add ground almond mixture and remaining 13 tablespoons melted butter; fold just to blend. Divide batter among muffin cups. Sprinkle tops with lemon peel and lime peel.

Bake cakes until golden and centers spring back when touched, about 20 minutes. Cool 5 minutes. Run thin knife around molds and invert cakes onto rack. *(Can be made 8 hours ahead. Cool; cover and store at room temperature.)*

Sprinkle tops of cakes with powdered sugar. Serve warm or at room temperature.

MAKES 12

Dark and White Chocolate Chunk Cookies

- 2⅔ cups bittersweet or semisweet chocolate chips, divided
- ¼ cup (½ stick) unsalted butter
- 2 large eggs
- ½ cup (packed) golden brown sugar
- 2 teaspoons vanilla extract
- ¾ cup self-rising flour
- ½ cup chopped crystallized ginger

- 3½ ounces high-quality white chocolate (such as Lindt or Perugina), very coarsely chopped

Preheat oven to 350°F. Line 2 baking sheets with parchment paper. Stir 2 cups chocolate chips with butter in heavy small saucepan over low heat until melted and smooth; cool 10 minutes. Beat eggs and sugar in large bowl until well blended. Beat in melted chocolate mixture and vanilla, then flour. Stir in ginger and remaining ⅔ cup chocolate chips; let stand 10 minutes.

Drop cookie dough by rounded tablespoonfuls onto prepared baking sheets, spacing cookies 1½ to 2 inches apart. Press white chocolate pieces into top of cookies, dividing equally. Bake until cookies look puffed and slightly dry on top, about 13 minutes. Cool cookies on sheets.

MAKES ABOUT 2 DOZEN

Pistachio Shortbread

- 1½ cups all purpose flour
- ½ cup plus 2 tablespoons powdered sugar
- ½ teaspoon salt
- ¾ cup (1½ sticks) chilled unsalted butter, cut into ½-inch cubes
- ½ cup natural unsalted pistachios, lightly toasted, chopped
- 1 large egg yolk
- ¾ teaspoon vanilla extract

Mix flour, powdered sugar, and salt in processor. Add butter, pistachios, egg yolk, and vanilla. Using on/off turns, mix until moist ball forms. Transfer dough to work surface. Divide dough in half. Form each dough half into 8x1¼-inch log (if dough is too soft, chill until firm, about 30 minutes). Wrap logs in plastic; refrigerate until firm, about 4 hours. *(Can be made 5 days ahead; keep chilled.)*

Preheat oven to 325°F. Slice logs into ¼-inch-thick rounds, rolling log after every few slices to retain round shape. Place rounds on ungreased baking sheets, spacing 1 inch apart.

Bake shortbread until barely golden, about 18 minutes. Cool shortbread on baking sheets. *(Can be made up to 4 days ahead. Store in airtight container at room temperature.)*

MAKES ABOUT 60

Peanut Butter and Fudge Brownies with Salted Peanuts

BROWNIES

- 3/4 cup (1 1/2 sticks) unsalted butter
- 7 ounces bittersweet or semisweet chocolate, chopped
- 3 ounces unsweetened chocolate, chopped
- 1 1/2 cups sugar
- 1 1/2 teaspoons vanilla extract
- 1/4 teaspoon salt
- 4 large eggs
- 1 cup all purpose flour
- 1 cup roasted salted peanuts, coarsely chopped

FROSTING AND GANACHE

- 1 cup chunky peanut butter (do not use natural or old-fashioned)
- 1/2 cup (1 stick) unsalted butter, divided, room temperature
- 3/4 cup powdered sugar
- 1/8 teaspoon salt
- 1/8 teaspoon ground nutmeg
- 1 tablespoon whole milk
- 1 teaspoon vanilla extract

- 7 ounces bittersweet or semisweet chocolate, chopped

FOR BROWNIES: Position rack in center of oven and preheat to 325°F. Line 13x9x2-inch metal baking pan with foil, leaving long overhang; butter foil. Place 3/4 cup butter in heavy large saucepan. Add both chocolates; stir over low heat until smooth. Remove from heat. Whisk in sugar, vanilla, and salt, then eggs, 1 at a time. Fold in flour, then nuts. Spread in prepared pan. Bake until tester inserted into center comes out with moist crumbs attached, about 30 minutes. Place pan on rack; cool.

FOR FROSTING AND GANACHE: Using electric mixer, beat peanut butter and 1/4 cup butter in medium bowl to blend. Beat in powdered sugar, salt, and nutmeg, then milk and vanilla. Spread frosting over brownies.

Stir chocolate and 1/4 cup butter in heavy small saucepan over low heat until smooth. Drop ganache all over frosting; spread to cover. Chill until set, about 1 1/2 hours. *(Can be made 1 day ahead. Cover and keep chilled.)*

Using foil as aid, transfer brownie cake to work surface; cut into squares. Bring to room temperature before serving.

MAKES 30

Index

Page numbers in *italics* indicate color photographs.

Acknowledgments

RECIPES
M. J. Adams
Bruce Aidells
Engin Akin
Alfama, New York, New York
Pam Anderson
Carolynn Angle, Standard Tap, Philadelphia, Pennsylvania
Scott Beattie
Bills, Sydney, Australia
Lena Cederham Birnbaum
The Back Bay Grill, Portland, Maine
Jimmy Bradley
David Burke
Canteen, San Francisco, California
Mary Cech
Melissa Clark
Hannah and Tim Cole
Giada De Laurentiis
Elizabeth Horton de Meza
Marissa Devins
Stefanie Dirienzo
Jill Dupleix
Lisa and Greg Dykstra
Lauren Fine
Janet Fletcher
Fruition Restaurant, Denver, Colorado
Rozanne Gold
Myra Goodman
Bill Granger
Dorie Greenspan
Jill Silverman Hough
Cheryl Alters Jamison and Bill Jamison
Amy Keller
Jeanne Thiel Kelley
Kristine Kidd
Evan Kleiman
Aglaia Kremezi
Josie Le Balch
Amber Levinson
Dave Lieberman
Jake Linzinmeir
Lori Longbotham
Susan Herrmann Loomis
Ryan Magarian
Janet Taylor McCracken
Tina Miller
Selma Brown Morrow
Alexandra Payard
Jamie Purviance
Gordon Ramsay
(Recipes taken from *Gordon Ramsay's Sunday Lunch*, published by Quadrille Publishing.)
Susan Reid
Matt Rice
Ristretto Roasters, Portland, Oregon
Tori Ritchie
Sarah Patterson Scott
Anita Sharp
Sibling Rivalry, Boston, Massachusetts
Mike Singer
SkyCity, Seattle, Washington
Mark L. Smith
Molly Stevens
Jessica Strand
Allen Susser
Sarah Tenaglia
Cynthia and Dwayne Thomas
Bret Thompson
Corinne Trang
26brix Restaurant, Walla Walla, Washington
Nick Vidargas
Violet, Santa Monica, California
Cindy & Ted Walter
Dede Wilson
Diane Rossen Worthington
Grace Young

PHOTOGRAPHY
Quentin Bacon
Noel Barnhurst
Wyatt Counts
Leo Gong
Yunhee Kim
Brian Leatart
David Loftus
Pornchai Mittongtare
Gary Moss
Ngoc Minh Ngo
Victoria Pearson
Scott Peterson
Con Poulos
Tina Rupp
Mark Thomas
Petrina Tinslay
Julie Toy